WAR IN EUROPE

Adolf Hitler's fanatical thirst for empire, the courageous resistance it provoked, and the titanic battles that ravaged a continent are now brought to breathtaking life in this remarkable new series by noted historian Edwin P. Hoyt. Here is the unforgettable story of World War Two in the European theater—a detailed, dramatic and astonishing military chronicle of victory and defeat in the brutal struggle between the forces of freedom and tyranny.

VOLUME FOUR

BATTLES IN THE BALKANS

VOLUME FOUR

WAR IN EUROPE

BATTLES IN THE BALKANS

EDWIN P. HOYT

AVON BOOKS ◆ NEW YORK

WAR IN EUROPE VOLUME FOUR: BATTLES IN THE BALKANS is an original publication of Avon Books. This work has never before appeared in book form.

AVON BOOKS
A division of
The Hearst Corporation
1350 Avenue of the Americas
New York, New York 10019

CONTENTS

PROLOGUE

With the Battle of Britain won by the British, and Adolf Hitler's mind focussed on the planned attack on Russia, early in 1941 the world's attention shifted from the air battles in Britain to two fronts in the war.

First was the Battle of the Atlantic. Hitler had wanted to drive the British out of the war, after failing in his attempts to bring them to the peace table with vague promises, by smashing their air defenses and invading the country. He failed in all this. The British remained obdurate and proclaimed that they would fight this war to a finish and win.

Some of the people around Hitler, particularly his navy men, believed that they could beat the British by starving them out. Thus Admiral Karl Doenitz stepped up his U-boat campaign in the spring of 1941, and Admiral Erich Raeder determined to use his major surface ships to terrorize British shipping in the Atlantic. Prime Minister Winston Churchill was more concerned about the German capability to destroy Britain's lifeline than any other aspect of the war. On this, Churchill and Doenitz agreed.

But the Atlantic battle in the spring of 1941 did not work out exactly as the Germans planned it.

The coming of the Italians into the war against Britain was hailed by Admiral Doenitz in the beginning, because the Italians had the largest fleet of submarines in Europe—a hundred in all, eighty of them ready to go into action. Since Doenitz then could put fewer than twenty U-boats to sea at one time, this looked like a real windfall to the German prosecution of the Atlantic war.

The Italians began in 1940 by working in the Atlantic off the Spanish coast and in the Mediterranean and they sank some British ships. Then the Italian submarine commander offered to bring boats to the North Atlantic to join with Doenitz's U-boats. Doenitz built a base for them at Bordeaux and the Italians brought up their fleet of submarines. Italian captains went to Wilhelmshaven and sailed with German U-boat skippers to see how the Germans worked.

Soon the Italians were given specific assignments by Doenitz's staff, and that is when the trouble began. The Italians did not seem to be able to get the hang of German U-boat operations. Their navigation was often faulty and when they radioed in a report of a convoy, usually the German wolf pack that would be sent out, could not find the ships. The Italian skippers sank some ships, but they found the sailing in the North Atlantic not to their liking. It was too cold and dismal and their submarines were not designed for this kind of work. They were too large, for one thing, unlike Doenitz's standard 500-ton U-boat. Their conning towers were too tall and cumbersome for the North Atlantic storms and they shipped enormous amounts of water when they dived in stormy weather. There were some exceptions. In one month, Commander Longobardo in the *Torelli* sank four ships, a record that would make a German captain proud. But by and large the performance was uneven by Doenitz's standards. The real reason, however, was that the Italian captains did not like to adhere to the German standard of discipline and Doenitz found them too unruly. The Italian captains were very brave, even foolhardy, in their adventurousness, but that was not what Doenitz wanted. He wanted strict attention to detail and discipline, and this was not the Italian way. After a few months, the experiment was abandoned by mutual consent and the Italians went their own way, concentrating their submarine activity in the Mediterranean.

In spite of this difficulty, the German submarine captains called the winter and spring of 1941 "the happy time" because they sank many ships. The British were at this time still woefully short of escort vessels. They were building the flower-class corvettes, but the first one had not yet been fitted out for sea. With the extension of the war into the Mediterranean, Britain had to send many convoys to Gibraltar, Alexandria, and Malta and they had to face the German and Italian submarines. In February 1941, the U-boats sank 290,000 tons of shipping, in cooperation with the Focke Wulff bombers of Hermann Goering's Luftwaffe. But in March, Doenitz lost five of his most skillful and experienced captains to the British escorts, and the heavy losses continued in the next three months. The fact was that the British were becoming better armed, and except for a brief period after the Americans entered the war, when the action was off the United States coast, the U-boats would never have such good luck again.

Quite apart from the U-boats, the German navy was conducting a war at sea with surface raiders. A number of these were fitted out in the earlier months of the war. The *Pinguin*, the *Kormoran*, and the *Atlantis* all went to sea. They looked like ordinary merchant ships, but they had heavy guns concealed behind their bulwarks, and many antiaircraft guns and depth charges. They were capable of remaining at sea for many weeks, and with the assistance of supply ships sent out to assist them, for months if necessary. They went as far afield as the Indian Ocean to sink many British ships.

But Admiral Raeder had even bigger plans. When Germany began to rebuild her navy secretly in the early 1930s, she not only concentrated on U-boats but on ships that could be used as raiders. Under the terms of the Versailles Treaty, she could build warships of 10,000 tons. The British and French regarded these as too small to be significant, but the Germans came up with a design for what were called "pocket battleships," which packed big guns and great firepower into a small, fast vessel. When the wraps were off and Hitler voided the Versailles Treaty, the German navy began the construction of much larger ships, such as the battleships *Bismarck* and *Tirpitz*. Six such vessels of 35,000 tons were planned, but by 1940 only these two were completed. The Germans also had several other very heavy ships, the *Scharnhorst*, the *Gneisenau*, and the *Prinz Eugen*.

In the spring of 1941, Raeder decided to use his heavy ships to break through into the Atlantic and increase the pressure on Britain's lifeline by raiding convoys on the North and South Atlantic runs. The *Scharnhorst* and the *Gneisenau* were sent to Brest, to await the coming of the *Bismarck* and the *Prinz Eugen*, which were at Gdynia in the Baltic, then the four heavy ships would sail into the Atlantic, a formidable squadron that would be a constant menace to British shipping. The problem was to get the *Bismarck* and the *Prinz Eugen* out of the Baltic Sea and into Brest on the Atlantic shore. It was impossible to think of trying to go through the English Channel. The Royal Air Force, British submarines, and the Home Fleet would pounce on the vessels and surely destroy them. The only way was to sail into the North Sea, up around the British Isles, and then break through into the Atlantic in the north, after which the two ships would steam to Brest.

So in the third week of May, when the battle for Crete was raging, the two ships arrived near Bergen, and anchored in a fjord for resupply. Two days later they were at sea, heading through the North Sea for the Denmark Strait and the Atlantic. They were spotted by an RAF plane just before they left Norway, but then they disappeared. Admiral Jack Tovey, commander of the British Home Fleet, was notified, and he put the fleet on alert. Gibraltar was also notified, and Force H., which was located there, sent the battle cruiser *Renown* and the aircraft carrier *Ark Royal* northward.

Admiral Luetjens, the commander of the German squadron, was flying his flag on the *Bismarck* and preparing for the sortie into the broad Atlantic for the raiding. The two ships remained undetected until they neared the Denmark Strait, and then two cruisers detailed by Admiral Tovey spotted them. The HMS *Suffolk* and the HMS *Norfolk* shadowed the German ships on the night of May 23, keeping Admiral Tovey informed about the Germans' position, speed, and course.

Admiral Tovey had two forces at sea, one which sailed from the base at Scapa Flow in the Orkney Islands and the other from the River Clyde toward Iceland and the southern exit from the Denmark Strait. The vanguard consisted of the fast battle cruiser HMS *Hood* and the new battleship *Prince of Wales*. The *Prince of Wales* was modern in every way, the newest battleship in the British fleet, but the *Hood* had been built at the end of World War I. In her case, speed and guns had been deemed most important, and although her hull was armored her deck was not. Thus she could keep up with the new fast battleship.

On the morning of May 24, guided by the messages from the *Suffolk* and the *Norfolk*, the *Hood* and the *Prince of Wales* came up on the two German ships. Admiral Luetjens sent the *Prinz Eugen* off for safety and opened fire on the British ships. One of the first shells from the *Bismarck* struck the deck of the *Hood*, pierced through and exploded in a magazine. The whole ship blew up and sank in three minutes, taking down all but a few men of her crew. The *Bismarck* then turned her fire to the *Prince of Wales* and damaged her seriously. But the *Prince of Wales* also damaged the *Bismarck* when one of her shells disrupted the oil system.

Admiral Tovey then decided to send an air attack against the *Bismarck* from the carrier *Victorious*. The attack came on the evening of May 24 and one torpedo scored a hit on the *Bismarck*, causing her to begin trailing oil. That night the *Bismarck* evaded the shadowing cruisers, Admiral Tovey then headed west into the Atlantic to make sure that he stood between the *Bismarck* and the convoy routes. But the *Bismarck* was making for Brest, not the western Atlantic. That night Admiral Luetjens radioed Brest, asking for quick repairs so he could keep his schedule with the other ships. The radio message was intercepted by the British, and although they could not read the German code, they got a fix on the transmission. And the next day, a search plane from the *Ark Royal*, coming up from the Mediterranean, spotted the oil slick and followed it to the *Bismarck*. The carrier launched an air strike which was unsuccessful, but later in the day launched a second air strike. Two of the *Ark Royal*'s torpedo planes were successful, and the torpedos disabled the *Bismarck*'s steering. She began to run in circles. Planes from the *Ark Royal* kept contact with the *Bismarck* all night. Admiral Tovey turned the Home Fleet around and headed for the area. The next morning he was on the scene with the battleships *Rodney* and *King George V*. Their 16-inch and 14-inch guns disabled the crippled *Bismarck*, and she was sunk by torpedoes from the cruiser *Dorsetshire*. She went down in twenty minutes, taking most of her crew, including Admiral Luetjens. That ended the most important threat to the British in the North Atlantic. The *Scharnhorst*, *Gneisenau*, and *Prinz Eugen* never did sail on their raiding voyage, and remained in Brest for many months until they ran the English Channel in a daring action and made it back to home waters.

So by the summer of 1941, the British were beginning to be victorious in the Battle of the Atlantic, after many vicissitudes.

The second important theater of action in the spring of 1941 was the Mediterranean. The war had been going on in Africa for many months, Benito Mussolini had launched a campaign to expand his African empire. All this was part of a plan by

Mussolini, who dreamed of making the Mediterranean into an Italian lake, to dominate its shores as the Romans had once done. The fall of France gave him designs on the French colonies, but his ambitions were not that limited. He also wanted the British colonies in Africa, and particularly Egypt and control of the Suez Canal. In the Balkans he wanted to control Greece, and had already invaded Albania. The Greeks were certain that Mussolini had designs to turn Greece into an Italian colony.

None of the Balkan nations wanted to be involved in the European war that began in 1939. They had formed a Balkan League to help keep them out of it, but almost immediately the League began to fall apart because of the various threats from German activity. The Germans wanted to be sure of the neutrality of Turkey if they could not induce the Turks to come into the war on their side, which by 1941 they knew they could not. When Hitler began planning for his attack on the Russians, suddenly Bulgaria, Rumania, and Hungary became important to him. He wanted to move troops through Rumania and Bulgaria to strike the Russians. So Hitler wanted these countries and Yugoslavia to join the Tripartite Pact of Germany, Italy, and Japan, which would make partners of the Axis. All these countries resisted to a certain degree, but by the spring of 1941, Bulgaria, Rumania, and Hungary had all fallen into line. The Yugoslav government indicated that it would also join the Axis, but there was a strong pro-British element in the country that resisted this course. At the same time that the Germans were moving diplomatically in the Balkans, so were the British, who tried to persuade the Yugoslavs into an alliance. Germany had no designs on Greece, which was an important trading partner for her, but here Mussolini had created complications.

In the summer of 1940, when Mussolini saw that France was about to collapse, he had declared war on Britain and France and sent troops into the Alps. The French had beaten the Italian army badly, and when the peace came, Hitler was not very sympathetic to Mussolini because Mussolini had delayed nearly a year in joining Germany in the war, so Mussolini did not get any French territory, or any monetary reparations from the French. His pride hurt, Mussolini invaded Greece, and almost immediately the Italian army was made to look ridiculous. In Africa he was losing the battles of East Africa and North Africa to the British, and by the spring of 1941 was in serious danger of being pushed out of Africa altogether.

Hitler was very annoyed with Mussolini's didoes, but he had to support his ally, and therefore his attention also turned to Greece. This was all the more true because in the spring of 1941, reversing a British policy of chilliness toward Athens, Prime Minister Churchill insisted that the British would have to guarantee Greek freedom and support the Greeks in any invasion by the Germans. Actually Hitler had no reason or inclination to invade Greece, other than the need to support Mussolini. In turn, Mussolini did not want Hitler to come in on the Albanian front. It would be too embarrassing to him. He had already at the end of 1940 reluctantly accepted a Hitler offer to help in Africa because the Italians were so obviously losing the battle. And so General Erwin Rommel had come to Africa in February after a meeting with Hitler and Field Marshal Walther von Brauchitsch. They told him that Mussolini's situation was critical in Africa and that he was to go to Africa with one light division and one Panzer Division, which would be named the Afrika Korps. He was to go immediately and get the lay of the land and the Fifth Light Division and the Fifteenth Panzer Division would be sent along shortly. The Italians would undertake the defense of Tripolitania in order to secure the space for the employment of the German Luftwaffe in Africa. The Italian forces were to be placed under Rommel, and he would report to Marshal Graziani. On February 11, Rommel flew to Sicily where the commander of the X Luftwaffe Korps told him of the latest losses of the Italians in Africa. The British had taken Benghazi and destroyed the last Italian armored division of the town, and they were about to advance into Tripolitania. Rommel had gone into action immediately, long before his troops arrived. He had asked the commander of the X Luftwaffe Korps to attack Benghazi that very night. A few German troops had arrived, and on February 24 the Germans first went into action in Africa.

Hitler was watching all this carefully. Admiral Raeder was delighted with the turn of events, for he believed that a victory in North Africa would bring Britain to her knees. He had never liked the plan for the invasion of Britain and was glad when it was abandoned. He now advocated a powerful drive in Africa, where he expected the Italian navy to be of great help. But so far the Italian navy had performed very poorly against the British Mediterranean Fleet.

In the spring the British and the Greeks were talking seriously about British aid, but Prime Minister Ionnis Metaxas rejected the first British offer as too insignificant to risk annoying the Germans. The British had offered only a few aircraft from the RAF and eventually some troop support, whereas Metaxas had wanted at least 100,000 men and an important RAF contingent. When Hitler learned of the negotiations of the British and the Greeks, he began thinking seriously of invading Greece, not only to help Mussolini, but to shore up his southern flank against British attack. Until he succeeded in defeating the Russians and taking over the South Russian oil fields, his only source of supply was the Ploesti fields of Rumania, which were quite close enough to Greece for the RAF to mount bombing raids.

In March, Mussolini asked Hitler to refrain from attacking Greece. He could handle the job, he said, and he was about to launch a spring offensive from Albania that would carry him all the way to Athens. But the March Italian offensive in Albania failed, even though Mussolini went personally to supervise the effort. And at the same time, the government of the regent Prince Paul of Yugoslavia, which had promised to join the Tripartite Pact, and had signed a treaty to do so, was overthrown in a coup and the treaty disavowed. Hitler was furious with the Yugoslavs for "betraying" him on the eve of his march into Russia. He decided to solve the problems of Yugoslavia and Greece simultaneously with a blitzkrieg campaign, and this resolve was strengthened when the British sent 60,000 troops and an RAF contingent to Greece. All that remained to be settled was the timing. It was necessary, Hitler said, to get the job done in a hurry, because he was forced to postpone the invasion of Russia from May 15 to June 22 and it would be dangerous to postpone it any longer and still try to defeat the Russians and occupy the Soviet Union before the winter snows fell.

So this was all part of the master plan, and the Balkan blitzkrieg was nothing but a necessary nuisance, this whole area regarded by Hitler as important only in the negative sense. Once Russia was conquered, then Hitler could again turn his full attention to the British and establish a Pax Germanica in Europe which would link up with Mussolini's dreams in the south, and might link up with the Japanese dreams in Asia. In that spring of 1941, General Richard O'Connor had been driving forward with the Fourth Indian Division and the Seventh Armored Division, which were piling up victories. But on the day after the battle of Sidi Barrani the Fourth Indian Division was withdrawn to go to East Africa, and the Sixth Australian Division took its place. This delayed actions for a time. Then came the demand from London for support for Greece, and on April 5 General Archibald Wavell was pressed by London into sending 60,000 British, Australian, and New Zealand troops to Greece. That was the last straw for Hitler, and the events depicted in this book then began to take place.

CHAPTER 1

The Italians Start a War

After the fall of France in June 1940, Italian dictator Benito Mussolini was bloodied but unbowed. He was bloodied because his attempt to invade France through the Alps in the last days had been a total failure, and his divisions had been so thoroughly defeated that when Hitler refused him the chunk of French territory that he coveted he could only whimper. Mussolini determined then that he would make a master stroke and recover the prestige lost in the Alpine adventure.

In July 1940, Hitler told Count Galeazzo Ciano, the Italian foreign minister and Mussolini's son-in-law, that Mussolini was to have a free hand in the Mediterranean, but he also cautioned Ciano against Italy's starting a Balkan war. In Rome the propaganda and press ministry began a campaign against Greece, accusing the Greeks of murdering an Albanian hero, who, in fact, was alive and a bandit wanted by the Greek authorities for many personal crimes. Before a week was out, Mussolini was talking about the price of peace for Greece: to give up to Italy Corfu and southern Epirus. But if the Greeks would not give up these territories, the Italian attack would begin.

The Greeks turned to the Germans, who were their best customers for Greek goods, and asked for help. But the Germans refused to interfere, and indicated that the Greeks should capitulate and join the Axis powers in the war as a sort of colony of Italy. The Greeks had asked the British for an alliance for many months, and the British had been cool to the idea. Many in Britain thought Greece was a bad risk, and in those days Winston Churchill was not in a position to effect relationships. So the idea of German alliance was very appealing to a little country that did not want to be involved in war. But the Germans were of no help, and meanwhile the Italian jackal was yapping at the door.

The Italian propaganda campaign became more violent. The Italians had occupied Albania in April 1939, after first giving King Zog an ultimatum. The Italian troops began to land in Albania a week later. Now it seemed apparent that they were going to use Albania as a point of departure to attack Greece. To emphasize the feelings, Italian soldiers in Albania had a new song:

> *"Andremo nell 'egeo*
> *Prendere purem il Pireo*
> *E tutto va bene*
> *Prenderemo anche Atene."*

> *"We will go to the Aegean*
> *We will then take the Piraeus*
> *And if all goes well*
> *We will also take Athens."*

The Italians then attacked the Greek navy without the slightest provocation. The new *Helle*, the Greek submarine that was the pride of the fleet, was anchored 800 yards off the pier at the island of Tinos on August 15, 1940. She was decorated for the Feast of the Repose of the Mother of God, a very important Greek Orthodox celebration. Suddenly she was burst by an explosion and two more explosions followed as torpedoes intended for her struck the breakwater. The Italians had torpedoed the submarine, and she went down that evening. A few hours later the Greek steamer *Friton* was attacked by Italian planes off Crete. Next day two Greek destroyers were attacked by a squadron of Italian planes, which bombed without result.

The day after the sinking, the Greek minister in Rome called on Count Ciano, who did not mention the *Helle*, but suggested that the Greeks would do well to settle the territorial question and give the Italians what they wanted. The Greeks did not reply. Mussolini was not yet ready to go to war. He was having troubles in East Africa and North Africa.

So he did nothing more at the moment, but continued to reinforce his troops in Albania.

Without telling his German allies, he assembled his troops for war across the Adriatic. On October 4, 1940, Hitler and

Mussolini met at the Brenner Pass in the Alps to discuss future military operations. Hitler spoke broadly about a "Continental Coalition" that would include Vichy France and Spain. France was to contribute her fleet to the operation. Reluctantly, because he was still smarting from his defeat by the French, Mussolini agreed to the plan. Mussolini then went back to Rome, talking to his intimates about occupying Greece. On October 13, he gave Marshall Pietro Badoglio orders to prepare for the attack on Greece. By this time the Italians had a large force in Albania, which they reinforced with another 40,000 men.

On October 15, Mussolini held a war conference in the Palazzo Venezia in Rome. Present were General Sebastiano Visconti Prasca and General Francisco Jacamoni, who were troop commanders in Albania. General Prasca said he saw no problem in starting the war from Albania. His forces outnumbered the Greeks by two to one, he said. Mussolini asked Prasca about Greek army morale and was given an encouraging answer about the Greeks. "They are not people who like fighting," he said.

Marshall Badoglio then spoke up. He said that he knew that Britain was too busy fighting in Egypt to give any significant assistance to the Greeks. Badoglio had big plans. All of Greece should be occupied by Italy, he said, including Crete and Peloponnesos. A force of twenty divisions would be required. It would require three months to reinforce the nine divisions and cavalry in Albania at the moment.

Mussolini said that was too long. He wanted to get into action. So it was decided that a strike would be made through the Epeirus to Athens, cutting Greece in half. About six divisions would be required to do this and two divisions and a battalion of carabinieri would keep watch along the Albanian frontier against Yugoslavia. Mussolini said he was ready to commit four hundred aircraft to the operation.

But this plan envisaged cooperation of the Bulgarians in the fight against Greece, and in the next few days, the Bulgarians, who were growing very nervous because of the many German demands on them, said they did not want to provoke the Turks, who might intervene on the side of Greece. So the Italian plan had to be scrapped and Mussolini had to start over again.

One of the reasons that the Germans were trying hard to prevent Mussolini from moving against Greece was that the

German foreign office believed that given a little time and encouragement, Prime Minister Metaxas would come around to the German side. Metaxas did not have any great faith in the British position in this war, and respected the Germans for their power. But Metaxas had very strong feelings against Italy and Mussolini. In fact, he had felt so strongly about that he had thought about provoking a war with Italy, but that would depend on British aid.

The British were shocked and upset by such an idea, which would only complicate their own war efforts.

So the Italians prepared for their war against Greece, with propaganda on the radio, with many air flights over Greek air space in open violation of international law.

The Greeks were very worried. At the end of October they appealed to the United States for assistance. But the Americans were not ready for involvement in the European war, and the evaluation of Washington was that the Greek situation was hopeless to begin with.

Meanwhile the Greeks were trying desperately to deal with the Germans and stave off war. The British would not have liked to hear the conversation of the German minister at Athens with a representative of the Greek foreign office on October 24. The Germans were told that the Greeks would give sympathetic consideration to the establishment of German bases in Greece for an attack on Egypt, if the Germans would keep Mussolini under control. But if the Italians attacked Greece, Deputy Foreign Minister Nichola Mavroudis said that any attempt by the Italians to invade Greece would be met with every resistance. The German minister responded by suggesting that the Greeks capitulate to the Italians, and thus avoid the war that threatened.

Greek agents in Albania were well aware of the Italian preparations for war. On the night of October 26 some information came from Rome to Theordoris Nikoloioudis, the Deputy Minister of Press and Information, that the Italian news agency had reported on "Greek armed bands crossing into Albania" and attacking Italian outposts. Prime Minister Metaxas was informed and he was in touch with General Alexander Papagos, the Greek army commander, who checked and concluded that these were attacks instigated by the Italians, using Albanian guerrilla bands.

On October 27, Mussolini, almost as an afterthought, announced to the Germans that he was going to invade Greece.

On the night of October 27, Emanuele Grazzi, the Italian minister to Greece, left the Italian legation to call on Metaxas at his home. It was about midnight, a strange time for a call. Grazzi and his military attache arrived at the prime minister's house in the Athenian suburb of Kifisiá, fifteen miles from the capital, at 2:50 on the morning of October 28. Metaxas had been in bed, and he greeted them in his nightshirt and dressing gown. The Italian minister presented him with an ultimatum. The Italian forces would begin to move into Greece at 6 o'clock in the morning. If the Greeks resisted . . .

The old Prime Minister had tears in his eyes as he spoke, in French. "*Alors, c'est la guerre*" ("Well, then it's war.").

Only if the Greeks resisted, said the Italian minister.

Metaxas pointed out that even if he wished to avoid war at all costs, there was no time for him to confer with the King or make the necessary arrangements to stop the Greeks from self-defense. The Greeks did not want war, he said, as he showed his unwelcome visitors out.

"*Vous êtes le plus fort. . . .*" he said. ("You are the stronger.")

The Italians left. They really had nothing else to say.

Mussolini did not even wait for a reply, but that night eight Italian units in Albania moved. Before dawn on October 29 they crossed the border into Greece, accompanied by the bombing of Greek cities.

Metaxas did not go back to bed after his Italian visitors left. He picked up the telephone and called the king and General Papagos, the commander of the Greek army. He told them that war was imminent.

At 5 A.M. Metaxas met with the cabinet. He told them what had happened and that Greece was going to fight. He asked them then if any of the ministers wished to resign their posts. The support was unanimous. Then, picking up his pen, Metaxas said, "God save Greece," and signed the orders for general mobilization.

Up until that moment, Metaxas had been the complete dictator of Greece. He held all the cabinet posts himself, and all the ministers were deputy ministers. But now he gave them full rein in their duties.

Later that morning, he and King George II toured Athens

and were greeted by the people with "unbelievable enthusiasm," as he put it.

Hitler and Mussolini met in Florence. Hitler was preoccupied with his plans for Operation Barbarossa, the invasion of Russia, and he was furious with Mussolini for undertaking this adventure. The Italian invasion of Greece was likely to provoke British intervention and the presence of British forces in Greece was the one thing Hitler did not want. One reason for the German plan to attack Russia was to secure the oil of the Caucasus, and until he had that supply, Hitler was dependent on the oil of Rumania. The British had already made guarantees to the Greeks. If Hitler threatened them they would come to Greece's assistance. Now Hitler's ally did threaten. If the British were established in Greece, it would be easy for them to bomb the Rumanian oil fields and thus to jeopardize the Russian adventure before it got started.

Instead of flying into one of his celebrated tantrums, Hitler concealed his anger, and promised Mussolini that the Italians would have German help if necessary to keep the British out of Greece. Mussolini said loftily that he did not expect to need any help, and predicted victory in Greece within two weeks.

But as Hitler feared, the British reaction to the Italian invasion was instant and strong. Immediately the RAF sent a bomber unit to Greece. Prime Minister Winston Churchill ordered more aid, and as a result, about half the British Royal Air Force strength in Egypt was sent to Greece within the week. The field commanders in Egypt did not like this diminution of their forces, but Churchill was playing a political game. Just then he was trying to woo Yugoslavia and Turkey to resist German demands that they join the Tripartite Pact of Germany, Italy, and Japan. By rushing to the aid of Greece, Churchill was giving reassurance to Yugoslavia and Turkey that he would do the same for them if they resisted the Germans.

On that first day, Prime Minister Metaxas gave a radio broadcast to the people of Greece.

"The time has come," he said, "for us to fight for the independence of Greece, for her integrity and honor. Now we shall show whether in fact we are worthy of our progenies and of the freedom our forefathers assumed for us. May the whole nation unite. Fight for the fatherland, your women and children, and for your sacred traditions.''

The king followed with an address in which he said he was sure every Greek would do his or her duty. Archbishop Chrysanthos of Athens called on the people to support the king and premier.

At nine-twenty that first morning of the war, the civilians of Greece were shown something of what war meant. Italian aircraft bombed the Piraeus, the Tatoi airfield outside Athens, and the city of Patras. The bombs were dropped from very high altitude and were not very effective.

On October 30, Metaxas called a press conference at the general staff headquarters, which had moved to the Hotel Grand Bretagne. He asked for the cooperation of the press in suppressing rumors. He spoke to them very frankly but forbade them to publish what he said.

As far as this war was concerned, he said, the decisive moment had come when the Italians invaded Albania. From that time on Italy's talk of peace had been empty talk and Italy had prepared for war. He said that he had known almost from the beginning that the Italians had sunk the *Helle*, but had suppressed the information in the interests of not antagonizing the Italians. Hitler had told him not to provoke them, he said. But had Greece allied herself with the Axis, he could have expected the British to seize Crete and other islands. And he expressed his confidence that ultimately the British would win this war against the Germans and the Italians.

At the end of the first week of fighting in Greece, the Italian advance had run out of steam and the Greeks were counter-attacking. They were carrying out what they called spur warfare, which they put into effect along the Iba or Metaxas Line. The object was to attack along the mountain spurs, seizing the summits and dominating the valleys. The defenders began to move along the heights parallel to the flanks of the Italian columns. The first Italian unit to feel the pinch was the third Alpine Division. The Greeks caught this unit in a valley, and attacked from the surrounding mountain spurs, using mortars very effectively. For a week they rained down fire on the enemy and caused that division to suffer almost 90 percent losses, going down from over 10,000 men to 1,000 by January. Mussolini's reaction was to fire General Prasca and replace him with General Ubaldo Soddu.

At first the world could not believe that the Greeks had successfully fought off the Italian army. The Italians had promoted their military forces as very strong. Greece was expected to collapse after offering token resistance, But the surprising news was confirmed after the first six days of fighting.

Mussolini's replacement of the commander of the Italian forces changed nothing. The Greek counteroffensive continued. On November 5, the *New York Times* suggested in an editorial that the dream might be possible. Six days later the *Times* said that the Greek successes had left the realm of wishful thinking and were reality. On November 11, the Greeks also stopped the Italian Siena Division, which had penetrated the Iba or Metaxas Line, by crossing the Kalamai River. On November 14, *New York Times* correspondent James Aldridge reported an eyewitness account of the decimation of the third Alpine Division at Métsovan Pass on November 13.

By that time the Greeks had mobilized 232,000 men in the two sectors in which they were fighting, and they outnumbered the Italians, although they did not have modern artillery, or tanks, or aircraft, except that which the British supplied.

The Greeks then began their assault on Koritza in the Macedonian sector. By November 21, the Greeks had driven the Italians back into Albania. They captured Koritza on November 22, and on November 30 captured Pogradeci on the east side of Lake Ohrid. On December 6, they took Saranda and Permeti. By January 6, they had penetrated into the enemy interior fifteen to twenty-five miles along the whole front.

The Greeks wanted to do more. They wanted to carry the war to the Italians in the air, but their Hellenic Royal Air Force was down to six aircraft. The British had promised them planes but had not delivered. The Greeks had to launch their offensive without air support. Finally the British began delivering some aircraft, but it was too little and too late. The real reason was that, aside from Winston Churchill, most of the British establishment had no faith in the Greek adventure from the beginning, and the military men, who were responsible for delivering the assistance that Churchill called for in such strident tones, simply were reluctant to act. Ultimately, the Greeks said, this behavior prevented their outright victory over the Italians. For example, the British had promised them trucks, and the trucks arrived on Christmas Day 1940 after much delay. But they had no tires. The tires did not come along for three months, and meanwhile the trucks were immobile, rusting away.

The reaction of the world was a surge of optimism in the democratic countries, which had become numbed by a succession of Axis victories and Allied defeats. The opposite reaction was seen in the Axis capitals. Rome and Berlin received the news from Albania and Greece with complete silence.

The Greeks were as surprised as anyone, for their small and inadequately equipped army was at first outnumbered fifteen to one by the Italians although, as noted, those figures changed as the fighting went on. The Greek plan from October 28 to November 14 was to fight a war of withdrawal along the Epeirus front to positions prepared on the Iba Line, which was twenty miles inside Greek territory. The Italian attacking force came to 125,000 officers and men. The Italians had committed also the 400 aircraft that Mussolini had earlier mentioned. The Greeks had about 35,000 men on the frontier. But the Greeks also had a larger force on the Iba Line, which had been set up to fight off an attack by the Bulgarians. When this attack did not materialize, the Greeks moved their troops up to fight the Italians, and this changed the odds. The hunters now became the hunted. The Italians should have attacked a month earlier, for now they faced very bad weather that hampered their every move.

It had all looked so easy when the Italian attack centered in the Pindus Mountains and Epeirus section. The Third Alpine Division was decimated, as noted, in the Pindus area. The Fifty-first Division led the move into the Epeirus. Both had been heading for Janina, the communications center for Epeirus and Pindus. From Janina it was 133 miles to Lárisa, and from there 204 miles to central Athens.

Whether or not this heroic defense would have succeeded if the British had given the aid they promised in good time is still debatable, because the real power lay in the hands of Hitler, who was very nervous about Greece. Hitler was watching events in Greece with increased perturbation. Hungary and Rumania were bulldozed into joining the Tripartite Pact, and the pressure was being put on the Bulgarians and Yugoslavs. Hitler was preparing his flanks for the assault on Russia. At the end of November it was no secret that Hitler intended to base troops in Rumania to assault Greece if necessary. This idea was not popular in Bucharest and some riots began. With the help of the Germans, Premier Ion Antonescu's Iron Guard put them down viciously.

On December 13, Hitler issued a directive to the German Wehrmacht to prepare for the invasion of Greece in case the British made it necessary. He would prefer not to get involved here, because it would divert efforts from preparations for Operation Barbarossa. He put the pressure on the German foreign office to secure his aims by negotiation. German Foreign Minister Joachim von Ribbentrop began to negotiate with the Bulgarian government to join the Tripartite Pact and permit transit of German troops through Bulgaria.

In January 1941, Mussolini was almost in despair. His military machine had failed completely in Greece. He started the New Year by ordering the chief leaders of the Fascist Party to Albania as regular officers. They all held commissions, which were largely sinecures. They included half a dozen cabinet ministers, even Mussolini's son-in-law, Count Ciano.

On January 10 Hitler invited Mussolini to Germany, and on January 18 the Italian dictator went to Berchtesgaden, the Hitler house near Munich. Hitler did not chide Mussolini for the disastrous Greek adventure. Instead, he said that if Britain began making threatening moves in Greece, he would attack Greece. In fact, he added, he was planning to join the attack on Greece in March.

Mussolini asked Hitler not to intervene. Given just a little more time, he said, he would bring off the victory, and there would be no need for Hitler to send troops into Greece. Hitler agreed to wait. He had been holding up the dispatch of General Rommel and a small experimental unit to North Africa to help the Italians turn defeat into victory. They agreed that Rommel would go. Mussolini would launch a new offensive against Greece in March.

On January 7, the British government, in the person of Foreign Secretary Anthony Eden, offered immediate assistance to the Greeks. On January 8, he sent General Archibald Wavell, the commander of British forces in North Africa, to Athens to talk about details and promised the Greeks monetary assistance, including $5,000,000 in American currency to buy military supplies from Turkey.

On January 15, Wavell was in Athens, and the meetings with Prime Minister Metaxas began. What became immediately apparent beneath all the rhetoric was that the British could make many promises but they could not deliver the goods.

Greek Prime Minister Metaxas knew something from his intelligence agents that the British government tried to conceal. Britain had such a heavy commitment in Africa that it could not possibly supply enough men and material to defeat Hitler in the Balkans.

What Metaxas needed was a hundred thousand men and arms to go with them. When it came right down to the facts, it was clear that all Wavell had to offer the Greeks was twenty-four pieces of field artillery, twelve heavy guns, forty antiaircraft guns, twenty-four antitank guns, and sixty-five light and medium tanks and no infantry. Metaxas also knew that the Germans just then had twelve divisions waiting in Rumania. So he rejected the British offers, because to accept them would be to invite Hitler to act.

So the British left Athens with promises of delivery of military supplies but no expeditionary force. As it was, the British had made so much noise about the whole offer that Hitler had the impression the British would move in Greece no matter what the Greeks wanted, and he planned accordingly.

Metaxas also assured the British that he would fight on. He had hopes of capturing Valona that spring, which would put an effective end to the Italian invasion. General Papagos submitted his list of urgent needs, and Metaxas forwarded them to Britain. The Greeks needed 1,500 trucks, 10,000 packhorses, 300,000 pairs each of boots and trousers, 200,000 each of jackets and overcoats. They would get about 10 percent of all this.

At the end of January, Prime Minister Metaxas died, and his successor, Alexander Koryzis, indicated he was more willing to accept limited British aid.

The British efforts were spurred by intelligence about German preparations in the area. By the middle of February, the German troops were pouring into Rumania, and soon there were 680,000 German soldiers who could cross the Rumanian border into the Ukraine on a 300-mile front between the Polish border and the Black Sea. The Germans, in turn, had intelligence that the British would soon move many troops from

Libya to Greece. Hitler now decided it was almost certain he would have to attack Greece to protect his Rumanian oil lifeline.

On February 22, British Foreign Secretary Anthony Eden came to Athens with General John Dill, the British chief of staff, General Wavell, and their staffs to talk seriously about British aid to Greece. They promised the Greeks about 100,000 men, naval support, and RAF support as soon as it could be managed. The Greeks indicated their willingness to fight the Germans. Strong efforts, including pleas from the United States, were invoked to try to bring the Turks around to support Greece, but the Germans won a diplomatic victory here, and the Turks refused to get involved.

Beginning on February 13, the Greeks made a serious military effort to capture Tepelena, on the Albanian front, which was the key to the capture of Valona. But by February 28, their initiative had failed. Now the Greeks were expecting the spring offensive that Mussolini had promised, so they were not about to move their troops out of the Albania area to the Aliákmon Line that the British wanted held as a defense against the Germans. By the end of the first week in March, it should have been apparent to the British military leaders that the Greek cause was lost before it was fought, and on the staff level it was. But on the political level, because of attitudes in America and elsewhere, it was necessary for the British to try to shore up the Greeks, and the Greeks, caught between the Germans and their real enemy the Italians, felt they had to fight, or have their country taken over by Italy. Turkey had deserted them and Yugoslavia was just about to sign a treaty with the Germans.

Mussolini was nearly ready to begin his offensive. He had transferred 350,000 men to Albania for the fight.

By the end of February, the German preparations for the attack on Russia were moving right along. Bulgaria had agreed to come into the pact, and German troops had moved onto Bulgarian soil, from which they would attack Russia.

To finish his preparations, what remained for Hitler was to deal with Yugoslavia and Greece, in order to assure that there would be no interference from them. On March 4, Prince Paul, the regent of the monarchy of Yugoslavia, was summoned to Hitler's eyrie near Munich and threatened that if Yugoslavia did not join the Tripartite Pact, the most dire consequences would result. If they did join, the Yugoslavs would be given the city of Salonika after it would have been taken away from Greece.

Prince Paul returned to Belgrade. He considered the problem: Yugoslavia must decide between Germany and Britain, and from what he could see the British had very little to offer. The future seemed to belong to Germany. Prince Paul began to talk to his ministers.

British General Maitland Wilson arrived in Athens early in March to arrange for the equipment of troops from the Middle East. The first convoy assembled in Alexandria and sailed. The troops arrived on March 7, and were cheered by the Greeks as they disembarked at Piraeus. But even as they came, the generals back in Cairo who were in charge of actual military operations knew that the Greek intervention by Britain would be a failure. Winston Churchill had promised too much, and he could not deliver it. The British Joint Planning Staff in Cairo began, in that first week of March 1941, to prepare for the evacuation of the British Expeditionary Force that was just arriving. The battle had been lost before it was even begun.

In Athens, General Wilson did not know it, but at that same time Mussolini was in Albania, where he had gone secretly to look over the situation. Hitler was prepared to act. His diplomats were putting the finishing touches on an agreement with the Yugoslavs that would keep them out of the Greek problem, and his troops were moving up to the Greek frontier of Bulgaria.

The great Italian offensive opened in Albania on March 9, and reached a peak on March 15. The Greeks were under assault by massive formations of troops supported by Italian aircraft. The British RAF, which was supposed to support the Greeks, was held in reserve against a German assault. The main Italian attack was in the Klisura-Tepelena area, where the Italians threw in thousands of men, especially to try to take Height 731. But they did not succeed. On March 15, General Papagos could announce that the Greeks had scored a victory. The Italian assaults would continue for another week, but they had no force. Mussolini left Albania on March 22, after requesting a truce. He had suffered 12,000 casualties. The Greeks had 5,300 casualties.

Hitler lost faith in Mussolini. Thereafter, anything the Italian dictator said about his military prowess was not to be believed in Germany. The preparations for intervention in Greece went on as quickly as they could be made.

On March 25, the prime minister and foreign minister of Yugoslavia signed the Tripartite Pact, in Vienna. But when they returned to Belgrade the government of Yugoslavia was overthrown by a popular uprising, and the young heir to the throne, Prince Peter, was declared to be king. This news was most unwelcome to Hitler. He flew into one of his rages and on March 27 called his military leaders to the chancellery in Berlin. He announced that this "betrayal" by the Yugoslavs meant that he now had to destroy Yugoslavia. He issued directive No. 25 for the war, which ordered the destruction of Yugoslavia with no notice and no diplomatic maneuvers. Marshal Goering was ordered to send the Luftwaffe from Hungarian bases to Belgrade to bomb. Hitler told Generals Keitel and Jodl, the chief of staff and operations director of the Oberkommandowehrmacht, to begin work immediately on plans to attack Yugoslavia. He announced to Ribbentrop that he was to tell Hungary, Italy, and Rumania that what had been Yugoslavia would be divided up among them.

Then he made what his generals called one of his basic errors of the war. In order to deal with Yugoslavia and the perceived threat of the British in Greece, he decided to postpone the invasion of Russia for four weeks. It had been scheduled for May 15, with the firm expectation that the war against Russia would be won before the snow fell. The four-week delay did not seem to him at the time to be a serious matter. More serious would be to leave his flank open to such enemies as the perfidious Yugoslavs.

General Jodl, the chief of operations of OKW, took the responsibility for drawing the plans. He had them finished by four o'clock on the morning of March 28. Hitler sent a message to Mussolini, asking—but really ordering—him to stop his military activity in Albania and screen the passes from Yugoslavia into Albania.

That same day, March 28, a large British convoy under Admiral A. B. Cunningham was at sea, bound for Piraeus. It included three battleships, one carrier, four light cruisers, and thirteen destroyers. They engaged an Italian foe and the battleship *Vittorio Veneto* was damaged and so was the cruiser *Pola*. The Italians sent the cruisers *Azra* and *Fiume* to help and they all were sunk, along with two destroyers.

The Yugoslav coup brought Foreign Secretary Anthony Eden back to Athens for another conference, which settled nothing. The Greeks moved troops up from the Aliákmon Line, toward the Yugoslav border, expecting the new Yugoslav government to come to their assistance in time of trial. General Wilson and Rear Admiral Charles Turle of the Royal Navy met with General Papagos, other Greek leaders, and the chief of the Yugoslav general staff at a village on the Yugoslav border to formulate plans that would include the Yugoslavs in operations against the Germans.

The talk was promising. The Yugoslavs would bring seventeen infantry divisions, three cavalry divisions and other units, totalling a million men. The Yugoslav Air Force now numbered 700 aircraft. But what was not said, and General Papagos knew, was that the Yugoslav forces were strung out all over Yugoslavia, and the air force planes were mostly obsolete. The plan looked good on paper, but Papagos was not convinced.

In the conference it became apparent that the British were not committing their forces in the way they were expected to, and that less than half the promised force had arrived. General Papagos emerged from the meeting with a sense of futility about the British efforts.

At dawn on April 6, the German armies were prepared to move. General Sigmund Wilhelm von List's Twelfth Army was the first to move, from southern Bulgaria into Yugoslavia. Meanwhile, Marshal Goering's bombers were concentrating on Belgrade with a thousand planes from Fliegerkorps IV and Fliegerkorps VIII. For three days the bombers came in at rooftop level. The Yugoslavs had no antiaircraft artillery, so it was easy picking. The city was to be destroyed by the bombers, burned and crushed, and 17,000 civilians were killed in the raids. Many more thousands were wounded, and the whole of Belgrade became a mass of smoking ruins. Hitler was pleased. "Operation Punishment," he called it.

The Yugoslav army was simply overwhelmed. The troops had been stationed all across the country, defending border points, and so there were not enough of them at any one point to put up serious resistance against the German panzer divisions. The Germans, Italians, and Hungarians came at them from all angles. General Kleist's First Panzer Group joined the

Twelfth Army forces, and the Second Army came in. All these included six armored and four motorized divisions. Against them the Yugoslavs could really employ only five of their thirty-one divisions.

In Greece, seven Greek divisions, the New Zealand Division, part of the Australian Sixth Division, and a British armored brigade prepared to withstand the German assault along the Aliákmon Line. But the key to the defenses was the Monastir Gap, the route from Yugoslavia into Greece, which was held by a mixed tank and infantry force. Other Greek forces were holding along the Metaxas Line in Macedonia. Altogether, the British had sent 53,000 men into Greece, far less than the 100,000 that Prime Minister Metaxas had demanded. From the outset of the Hitler movement, such responsible Greek leaders as General Papagos had the feeling that the Greeks were fighting for honor, and for honor alone. Given the forces at hand, there was no way they could win against the Germans.

CHAPTER 2

The Germans Strike

At five-forty on the morning of April 6, 1941, which was Palm Sunday, the German minister to Greece visited the foreign office and announced that Germany was going to invade Greece to wipe out the British threat to Germany and her allies. Already the German panzers were moving into Yugoslavia. Even before the news of the German invasion was released by the government at 8:00 in the morning, crowds had begun to gather in the streets of Athens. Soon they had the sobering news that the Yugoslavs, on whom many Greeks had counted for assistance, were the object of a particularly frightful campaign, and that Belgrade was already burning.

Athens did not have long to wait. By nine-thirty, German bombers had assembled over the port of Piraeus. The Stuka dive-bombers concentrated on the docks and ships. Other bombers laid mines in the approaches to the port. When this first air attack ended two hours later, about 60,000 people were homeless and moving to Athens for shelter. The port was badly damaged.

Laird Archer, an American resident, watched from his window in the suburb of Psychico that night as the German bombers came again at about 11 P.M. and the antiaircraft guns opened up and searchlights sent their beams into the sky. "The air quivered with the grunt of explosions and the clatter of rapid fire like a stick drawn along a picket fence," he said. Later he learned that in the night raid, a British tanker had been hit first, which then set fire to the ship *Clan Frazier*, which was loaded with munitions. A British destroyer came in and tried to tow the munitions ship out to sea. The towline kept breaking, but finally the destroyer got the ship outside the Piraeus breakwater, where it exploded. Houses and buildings in the immediate area were flattened, but Piraeus itself was saved.

Archer was awakened the next morning at 4 A.M. by renewed German bombing. That day news began to come to Athens about events in Yugoslavia. It was bad. The Germans had moved quickly twenty-five miles into Yugoslavia, and found that the Yugoslav resistance was disorganized. Belgrade was in ruins that second day, with the government moved to Sarajevo.

Athens was talking about the brave defense of a fort in the Struma Pass northeast of Salonika, which was attacked by German panzers and aircraft. Ten tanks were disabled and six planes shot down by the defenders, who finally had to sacrifice the fort, but not before the last 150 volunteer defenders were killed. The forts of Istimbey and Kelkaya held out to the last, and two forts still stood, blocking German passage through the narrow gorge.

The newspaper *Estia* paid tribute to the brave defenders.

"Greeks, you have in front of you pages of Greek history written yesterday and the day before and again being written today. Officers and soldiers who remained in their forts to the end, blocking even with their bodies the passage of the enemy. They knew their fate as early as a month ago. They realized that they had to withstand the first shock of the attack without support and with no expectation of rescue. They asked to be given this hopeless task. They sent what they had to their families, partook of their last communion, and wrote the last letters, one of which says: 'With our fingers on the trigger, we are following the movements of the enemy, expecting the ultimatum with the resolution to die and with the certainty that we will show the Germans what being a free Greek means.'"

The Greeks were thoroughly aroused, and urging their soldiers on. Princess Frederika of the royal family, visiting a military hospital, was stopped by soldier with one leg. He begged her to get him sent back to the front. "I can still shoot," he said.

The use of Piraeus as a port ended when the Germans announced that if the British used it, they would bomb Athens.

The Greeks and the British assembled their defenses. The Greek Fourteenth and Eighteenth Divisions were assigned to the Metaxas Line on the Bulgarian frontier, along with the Nestos Infantry Brigade. The first Aliákmon Line facing Yugoslavia, in western and central Macedonia, was to be defended by the W Force, a combined British-Greek force commanded by General Wilson. The Greeks contributed two infantry divisions, the Twelfth and the Twentieth and the Nineteenth Motorized Division, which was equipped mostly with captured Italian equipment and vehicles, including twenty-five Italian tanks. The British contingent was the Second New Zealand Infantry Division, the Sixth Australian Infantry Division, and the First Tank Brigade of the Second Armored Division. The Polish Infantry Brigade and the Seventh Australian Division had been promised, but at the last minute, because of the threat from Rommel to Egypt, they had been ordered to remain in Egypt.

The Greeks also had fifteen divisions on the Albanian front, holding against the Italians. But General Papagos decided not to move any of them. The troops were exhausted after defeating the Italian spring offensive, and Papagos did not have the transport to move them anyhow.

So with these forces, General Wilson was supposed to fight eleven strong German divisions under German Twelfth Army commander General von List. The air power discrepancy was even worse than that on the ground. The British had some eighty aircraft. The Germans had 800 based in Rumania and Bulgaria, and the Italians had another 300. From the outset, the Germans and Italians had control of the air, and although one British RAF pilot shot down thirty-five enemy planes over Greece before going down himself, the Greeks and the RAF were completely overwhelmed in the air.

The Metaxas Line on the Bulgarian frontier was the first area in Greece to meet the blitzkrieg. By nightfall on the first day, the Second and Seventh German panzer divisions had swept through the southeastern corner of Yugoslavia, turned south and seized the Greek town of Doiran. On April 8, the Germans overran the Greek Nineteenth Motorized Division, and moved to outflank the Metaxas Line and take Salonika. On April 9, the Germans entered the town unopposed. That day the Greek Army of Eastern Macedonia surrendered to the Germans under orders from Athens.

Thursday, April 9, was a black day for Greece. Salonika had fallen and Piraeus was burning. General Papagos reported to General Wilson that the Yugoslavs were incapable of giving any assistance. Part of General von Stumme's XL Corps had entered Skopje in Yugsoslavia and was expected to turn into central Macedonia and hit the Monastir Gap at any time.

The Metaxas Line continued to hold. The Germans continued to bomb Piraeus, Daphne, and Phaleron Bay. Laird Archer and his friends continued to watch the bombing.

"We went to our usual vantage point on the terrace roof until the attack drove us indoors to the laundry window to watch the bombs punctuating the moonlight, interrupted by sharp snappy flashes of the tracers. Deep quaking bl-l-umps of bursting bombs kept us worrying over the fate of the large British convoy in the bay but we reassured ourselves that the sound was just as heavy when the bombs struck only the sea. How expert we have grown but how helpless we feel. We shouted in barbaric glee at the flaming feathers spiraling slowly down to betoken two bombers caught almost simultaneously. Later a third added to our satisfaction and nobody thought of the men trapped and charred within those flaming chariots. They are no longer men to us but beasts that threatened the little homes and panic stricken population of the refugee settlements along the shore . . ."

The Greeks who manned the Metaxas Line fought valiantly. They were 15,000 strong. The German frontal attack was led by the Seventy-Second Infantry and the Fifth and Sixth Mountain Divisions supported by German aircraft. It took the Germans three days to penetrate the line, and then they did it with finesse, not force. The German Sixth Mountain Division crossed a 7,000-foot mountain range through snow, and broke through the line at a point that had been declared to be inaccessible. On April 10, the Fourteenth and Eighteenth Greek divisions surrendered officially, but small units continued to fight, and the Germans had to reduce each position by enveloping attacks supported by aircraft. The fighting continued on that line until April 19, and then the German 125th Infantry Regiment suffered so many casualties that it had to be withdrawn.

On April 14, the Greek public showed some optimism when it was learned that the forces in northern Greece had pushed the Adolf Hitler Division back with heavy losses. The good news elsewhere was that Haile Selassie had been returned to his throne in Ethiopia, and was promising to raise an army to help the Allies. The bad news was that the Germans were being replaced in France by Italian troops, which meant that more Germans would be thrown into Greece.

The Germans did not really need any more troops. On April 9, General von List ordered his troops to breach the Aliákmon Line. They were to drive from Salonika west toward Edessa. The XL Panzer Corps was to move south through the Monastir Gap heading for Kozáni. By April 15, they cut into the gap above Edessa and were pushing down on Kozáni between the 5,000-foot spur above Mount Olympus and the 6,000-foot Mount Vernon range.

To add to the Allied difficulties, they fell out among themselves. How much difference it would have made is debatable, but the mutual distrust that developed between the British and the Greeks meant they did not really communicate, and their cooperation was only skin deep. The fighting in central and western Macedonia between April 9 and April 13 became an uncoordinated withdrawal in the face of a superior enemy. On April 10, the First SS Regiment entered Flórina and swung east toward the village of Vevi, where they met the British for the first time. The British fought at Vevi, and four miles south, two Australian battalions, a New Zealand battalion of machine guns, and a Ranger Battalion tried to stop the enemy at Kleithi Gap. The Australians held the heights overlooking the pass road. But the enemy was very strong and had the air power to make the difference. Fighting in rain and snow, the Australians had to give way. They began to retreat by night over rough roads to avoid the German aircraft. In Athens, by April 11 the government and public morale had begun to crack. General Papagos had all he could do to keep shoring up and moving the Greek positions in order to keep up with the British retreat. King George, who was reluctant to interfere in matters of state, suddenly realized that he had to take a strong position. He declared that the Greeks would not, as some rumors had it, declare a separate peace within the Axis powers. He would continue the war from abroad until the Axis was defeated. But in the government offices in Athens, all the talk was now about getting out. The Greek navy was working with the British to transfer the navy to Crete, and on April 12, the king suggested that the seat of the Greek government be moved to the British colony of Cyprus, and the Greek navy transferred to Alexandria.

The new British position was to extend from the town of

Platamon on the Gulf of Salonika west along the north side of
Mount Olympus, then to the bridge over the Aliákmon River
northwest of Servia and then along the mountains on the western side of the Kozáni-Amyntaion valley. But the Germans
managed to intercept General Wilson's orders and increased
the speed of their pursuit. Perhaps even worse, the British
could provide only a hundred trucks for the retreat, to move
two Greek divisions.

By April 13, they were retreating toward Kozáni. The British
First Armored Brigade covered the withdrawal. Brigadier S. H.
Charrington, commander of the force, selected a position between Vevi and Kozáni south of Ptolemaís. On April 13, the
British fought their first major battle of the Greek campaign
against the Germans. The Thirty-third German Panzer Regiment attacked, supported by the inevitable aircraft. The First
Armored Brigade, assisted by Rangers and two companies of
the New Zealand machine gun battalion, destroyed several
German tanks, but by nightfall the position was untenable, and
they had to abandon thirty-two tanks which had trouble with
their tracks.

The withdrawal left the Allies with only a few tanks. Some
of the men were without weapons. And there was no peace
for them at Kozáni. On the night of April 13th, the Germans
were approaching the town.

Laird Archer and his now-extended family, which included
several refugees from northern Greece, watched the bombing
around Athens every night. They saw five German planes shot
down on the night of April 16. The Stukas had sunk two ships,
but the ships had already been unloaded, so all was not lost.
The Greeks seemed to be still hopeful. As long as the British
continued to arrive, they would remain that way.

Athenians knew that the Germans were forcing their way
forward at Sarantaporon Pass and at Kalabáka Pass. At the
latter place, the British and Greek lines joined, and the Greeks
were holding as the German tanks came at them, destroying
one tank after the other. But there were too many tanks. In
Athens the people began to realize that the gallant struggle was
doomed.

The Germans now had forty divisions to commit and the
Italians had thirty. The British had 60,000 men, and the Greeks
had 300,000. In weight of sheer numbers, there was no way
the Allies could defeat the Axis here. Some of the Greek

ministries were already burning their official papers, lest the Germans get them. What was it all going to mean, this continuation of the fight? King George and Prime Minister Koryzis were determined to delay the Germans and upset their timetables. They had already done that.

On April 17, the Germans crossed the Aliákmon River near the sea and southeast of Salonika.

The Greeks were trying to make a defense at Klisoura Pass, for if Klisoura fell the Germans could then outflank the British force by moving south and east to Grevená. On April 13, the Germans met stout resistance from the Greeks, but the next day the Seventy-third Infantry Division forced the Greeks to give ground. The Germans occupied Kozáni that day, and the position at Klisoura Pass was outflanked. On April 15, the Germans reached Grevená, and the Greek position in Albania was threatened.

The Greeks were really already withdrawing from Albania on orders of General Papagos, with the Italians following very cautiously. There were no troop engagements with the demoralized Italians, but Italian and German aircraft assaulted the retreating Greeks constantly during the daylight hours. On April 13, General Wilson had decided to withdraw to the Thermopylae Line, a hundred miles to the south, but he said nothing to the Greeks, who were still holding the Klisoura and Pisoderian Passes. On April 15, the withdrawal began. Just before dawn that day, almost all of what was left of the British Royal Air Force was destroyed in a dawn air raid that caught the British Blenheim bombers and Hurricane fighters on the ground at two forward airfields and destroyed sixteen bombers and fourteen fighters. All aircraft were ordered out of the forward areas, and there was no more air support at all.

In Egypt, the British high command was already executing the plan for evacuation of British forces from Greece.

On April 16, General Papagos met General Wilson in Lamía to review the military situation. For the first time, Papagos then learned of Wilson's decision to withdraw to the Thermopylae Line. He objected that to do so would be to open the road for the Germans to isolate the Greek forces of the Army of the Epeirus. Then they discussed the political situation.

"When is the government leaving for Crete?" asked General Wilson.

"I don't know," said Papagos. "What do you think?"

"I believe you should leave as soon as possible," said General Wilson.

"I agree," said General Papagos.

And the two generals agreed that the British had to be evacuated to fight again in this war. Papagos favored this course so that the destruction by the Germans could be minimized, for it was apparent that the Germans must win this unequal struggle. All that remained to be settled was when and how many more men would die, and how many more cities, towns, and villages would be destroyed.

Already the king had decided to evacuate his government to Crete, and the government was moving. With this, an incipient revolt against authority began. Minister of War Nicholas Papadimas issued an order to the army to stop resisting, and said the government was leaving Greece. An hour later his action was disavowed by the prime minister. In the Albanian sector, two of the Greek generals were eager to surrender and get the war over with, but Papagos and the king refused their entreaties. Greece would not surrender, said the king. Greece would fight on.

On April 16, the Germans were moving so rapidly through Flórina, Kastoria, and Grevená that they threatened to cut off the retreat of the British, and the government.

On April 18, the question of capitulation was discussed in the cabinet meeting, and again the king refused to consent. He had just received an estimate from the British that they could hold the position for four more weeks. Papagos was called in to answer questions, and he confirmed the fact that morale on the Albanian front was gone, but he did not say that the British could not hold.

That day the prime minister learned of treason within his cabinet. He and the king had earlier approved an order giving extra Easter pay to the troops. When the order was issued by Papadimas, he had amended it to say "and leave," and sent this version to officers and men holding the left center of the line against the Germans. When the order came to the front, many officers and men refused to leave. But some did, enough so that the Germans were able to break through and take Kalabaka Pass. All this was unknown in Athens until the eighteenth, when a group of four officers brought their copies of the order directly to the royal palace and showed them to the king. The king immediately called Koryzis, who summoned the cabinet and the high command. In front of them, he accused the minister of war of treachery, and canceled the plans for the government to move to Crete. He dismissed the council and then went to report to the king. Having done so, he went home and locked himself in his study without speaking to his wife.

The king had worried after Koryzis left the palace, and sent emissaries to his house to see that everything was all right. The palace men arrived, but as they knocked on his door they heard two shots. They broke down the door and found the prime minister dead on his bed, with an icon of the Mother of Christ on the bed beside him. He had taken his own life to escape the dreadful responsibilities thrust on him.

The minister of war and the minister of the navy, who was also in on the plot, had left the cabinet meeting and driven swiftly to the port of Chalcis where they ordered a motorboat to take them north along the coast, intending to make contact with the Germans. The commander of the port refused to give them a boat. The war minister stormed at him.

"Don't you know who this is that is giving you the command?" he said.

"Sir," said the port commander, "I take orders only from our king."

In spite of the blustering, the two ministers were then arrested and brought back to Athens to await trial for treason.

At this point, a reluctant King George II decided he had to take over the government of Greece. He asked two political leaders to form a government, but they failed to get unity on the question of whether Greece should fight on. Finally Vice Admiral Alexander Sakellarious, chief of the naval general staff, managed to organize a government. King George would be prime minister.

On the day of the funeral of the former prime minister, General Wavell arrived in Athens to assess the military situation and review his already-made decision to evacuate the British forces. But in London there was a different view. Prime Minister Churchill wanted to bleed the Germans as much as possible, and hoped that the British and Greeks could hold for a few more weeks. The reason was his desire to win a victory in Libya, where Rommel was on the offensive. Every day that the German air force remained in Greece made a difference in Libya.

But General Wavell had already decided on evacuation, and nothing he saw or learned in Greece changed his mind. The British naval representative with his party had already sent a message to Cairo asking for ships to begin arriving at Greek evacuation ports on April 18.

By this time the Greek defense agency was in shambles, with some generals trying to subvert the government and secure an immediate surrender. But by April 20, it did not make too much difference, because the Greeks were defeated. King George refused to surrender, and on April 20 took over as acting president of the council of state, but reports made it clear that the battle was lost. The king spoke to the people of Greece that night on the radio appealing for faith and confidence. But the air raids on Athens told the story: On April 21, the city was raided six times. And two Greek armies surrendered to the Germans, but made it clear they were not surrendering to the Italians. When Mussolini learned that the Greeks had surrendered to the Germans without anyone telling him, he was furious, and telephoned Hitler to demand Italian participation in the surrender. Hitler then ordered that the surrender terms would not become effective without *Mussolini*'s approval. The Greeks continued to fight the Italians in Albania until April 23. The surrender, which now included the Italians, was signed in Salonika on April 23. Even to the last, the Greeks would not surrender to the Italians, and one regiment on Corfu surrendered to a group of three German officers.

When General Papagos learned of the surrenders, he fired the generals involved, but it was too late to change matters. King George, the royal family, and most of the cabinet left for Crete on April 23. On that day, the Australians and New Zealanders, now known as the Anzac Corps, took positions along the Thermopylae Line 150 miles north of Athens. This was the place where in 480 B.C. the Spartans had fought the Persians to keep them from overrunning Athens. The Anzacs had reached it after an orderly but difficult retreat. Here is how it was described by one Australian writing to the *London Times*:

"For two days I have been bombed, machine gunned, and shot at by all and sundry. German Stukas have blown two cars from under me and strafed a third. All day and all night there have been waves of Germans in the skies. Eighteen Messerschmitts strafed us on the road last evening. Bullets ripped the trucks and one was destroyed, but nobody was lost except the truck. Before that, the convoy I was in was attacked seven times in two hours, but not once was the convoy disorganized or broken up. The Germans are using a fantastic amount of aircraft, more than I ever saw in Norway under similar conditions of terrain. Goering must have a third of his air force operating here and it is bombing every nook and cranny, hamlet, village and town in its path.''

The Germans began to approach the Thermopylae line, but they did not have enough forces in hand for an attack until April 24. On that day the Luftwaffe began the attack on the gun positions of the Nineteenth Australian Brigade, which was holding Brallos Pass. The Germans then sent their panzers in, but the Australian line held.

General von Stumme, the German commander, then switched his attack and moved his panzers against the Sixth New Zealand Brigade farther east. The New Zealanders fought off wave after wave of Germans, and their artillery knocked out many German tanks. But at the end of the day, the Anzac Corps was ordered to withdraw. The New Zealand Fourth Infantry Brigade served as the rear guard. The British were on their way to the ports, to evacuate Greece.

It was essential that the Peloponnesus be held. The bridge across the Corinth Canal was secured, and on the twenty-fourth a team of New Zealanders prepared the bridge for demolition. The Anzacs continued to retreat over the bridge on the twenty-fourth and twenty-fifth.

Not only were the troops moving out, but in Athens the foreigners who could get out were leaving. But the Germans were bombing anything that appeared in Piraeus harbor. On April 25, they bombed the SS *Hellas*, a former Vanderbilt yacht that was serving as a hospital ship, and killed most of the 250 British wounded, 580 women and children, and 170 civilian men. Two Greek hospital ships, the *Andros* and the *Politkos*, were also sunk that day. The British troops who marched through Athens on their way south were cheered by the Greeks, even as the Germans dropped leaflets warning the people to stay away from the sea, because the bombers would be going after the British. That night the remainder of the government and the British military leaders left by flying boat for Crete.

On the morning of April 26, German paratroops landed

around the Corinth Canal bridge and tried to seize it, but were driven back by the Anzacs, giving the British forces a few more hours to complete the evacuation.

On Sunday, April 27, the Germans entered Athens and raised the swastika above the Acropolis. By this time, almost all of the British who would get out were gone or going. In all, more than 50,000 of the 62,000 who had been sent to Greece were evacuated in these last few days. Some of the others were casualties. Some had left earlier, some were hidden by the Greeks and later escaped, but most were to become prisoners of war.

On April 29, Germans entered the port of Kalámai on the southern tip of the Peloponnesus, and the evacuation was over. Now the battle would turn to Crete.

CHAPTER 3

Defense of Crete

Long before the disaster in Greece, it was plain that the British High Command did not have a plan for the war in the Mediterranean and was acting in response to the Germans and the Italians.

General Wavell had been forced by Prime Minister Churchill to give up a winning position in North Africa. By the winter of 1941, the Italians had been defeated and all but pushed out of Libya, and another successful drive would have done it. General Erwin Rommel said as much when he arrived in February to stiffen the Italian position with a small panzer unit. But because of Churchill's insistence, the advantage in North Africa had been cast away. The troops and planes that would have enabled General Richard O'Connor to win a decisive victory in the desert were wrenched away to Greece, where from the beginning the Greeks knew there was no way that such a small force could affect the outcome if the Germans attacked. And the British presence made it certain that the Germans would attack. From the outset in the fall of 1940, the Greek adventure was a British disaster which set back the British war effort in the Mediterranean by almost two years.

To make matters worse, only when it became apparent that the Greek disaster was upon them, did the British really do anything to defend Crete. This failure must be blamed on General Wavell and his staff, because from London Prime Minister Churchill had ordered the buildup of the defense of Crete and believed it was being undertaken, when in fact it was not.

The first inkling to the British that Crete was worth worrying about came on October 29, 1940, when the Italians started their war against the Greeks. Suddenly Churchill remembered Crete, and decided that Britain must undertake its defense to prevent the Italians from securing it and making an air base of it. The first British force went ashore at Suda Bay on Crete, taking in twenty antiaircraft guns and some naval guns for shore defense. Churchill then declared in a message to Foreign Minister Anthony Eden, who was in the Middle East, that "establishment of a fueling base and airfield in Crete to be steadily developed into a permanent war fortress is indispensable." Speaking to General Ismay, his military aide, Churchill said he would like to see Suda Bay developed into a second Scapa Flow, and made as impregnable as that naval fortress strengthened by the British after the sinking of one of their battleships there by a German U-boat at the outset of the war. His concept was that the navy would develop a stout defense there, but that the army should maintain several thousand men, and that the Cretans should have at least a division of troops which the British would train. "To lose Crete because we had not sufficient bulk of forces there would be a crime," Churchill said.

Had Churchill been paying attention to the Royal Air Force and the Joint Planning Staff in London he might have been dissuaded entirely from the Greek adventure. In November, the RAF had declared that the basis for the defense of Greece should be Crete, which should be held at all costs.

By the end of November, Churchill was confident that his wishes were being carried out. But General Wavell had many other matters on his mind. One was Churchill's insistence on reinforcing Greece, which was robbing Wavell of the troops he wanted to fight in North Africa. Another was the defense of Malta, which had scarcely been started. So Wavell did not in fact pursue the matter of Crete defenses. He and Anthony Eden agreed that Crete did not seem to be in any particular danger, since the Italians were already beginning to lose in Albania and western Greece. But when they so said to Churchill he did not agree, and he wanted to know just what was going on at Crete. "I hope to be assured that many hundreds of Cretans are working at strengthening the defenses and lengthening and improving the aerodromes," he wrote.

But in fact no such activity was going on, and the months passed. No plan was devised for the defense of Crete. The local people were not mobilized to build defenses. London remained unaware that its wishes were not being carried out.

Then, on March 31, came disaster in North Africa that diverted all attention. Rommel had assembled his slender resources swiftly, and against orders from Berlin, he started an offensive that drove the British back from Benghazi to the Egyptian frontier, isolated Tobruk, and resulted in the capture of Britain's best African field general, Richard O'Connor. Then came a revolt in Iraq which forced Wavell to send an infantry brigade and a regiment of artillery he could ill afford to sacrifice at the moment. In April came the German invasion of Greece, and Wavell was also involved in Syria against the Vichy French. Crete was forgotten in the excitement.

Between November, when Churchill began planning, and April, the command of the island changed six times. The first commander, Brigadier Tidbury, looked over the island and saw the needs. What he saw was an island 160 miles long and about thirty miles wide, which lies east and west across the outlet from the Aegean Sea, two hundred miles south of Athens. A high and rugged mountain range runs from end to end of the island, the tall peaks concentrated on the southern end where the cliffs fall into the sea. On that southern shore there was no harbor. In fact, there was only one harbor of any importance on the whole island. Palaiokhóra on the west and Sfakia and Tymbaki on the east were fishing ports, but they could be used only by small boats. The real harbor was located at Iráklion on the northern coast. It could accomodate vessels up to 3,000 tons at its docks. At Suda Bay, seventy miles to the west, there was virtually nothing, while at Canea, across the Akrotiri Peninsula, the ancient quays that went back to the days of the Venetians could take nothing but small boats. Between Canea and Iráklion the town of Réthimnon had a facility, but here, thirty miles east of Suda, ships could discharge their cargoes only by lighter.

A modern airfield had been constructed at Iráklion. Ten miles west of Canea, at Maleme, there was an unfinished runway. At Réthimnon a narrow landing strip had been built six miles east of the town. Work had begun on a fourth airfield in a valley southeast of Iráklion.

Along the northern coast of the island farmers cultivated strips of land between the foothills of the mountains and the beach. One area of this sort stretched between Maleme and Suda. The mountain ravines ran down to the pebbled beach.

At Suda the narrow bay divided the mainland from the Akrotiri Peninsula, with the harbor at its western tip. Two miles away, Canea faced north across the Aegean Sea.

The only paved road on the island ran east and west between the northern towns. Most of its bridges were too weak to take heavy traffic such as tanks. The roads that ran north and south were little more than cart tracks. One other track that could be managed by vehicle traffic ran through the mountains toward Sfakia but ended a mile and a half above the port. There were no railroads and no facilities for telephone and telegraph.

Brigadier Tidbury had assumed that the assault would come from the air, and the enemy would try to capture the airfields with the ports and to block movement on the roads and communication with the island. What could have been done was to build landing facilities at the southern fishing ports, improve the roads leading north, build fighter airstrips in the south, and mine the airfield of the north, and arm the Cretans. Later, General Wavell said there were very few Cretans on the island, that most of them had been sent to fight in Albania. But this was not true. There were 400,000 Cretans on the island and 15,000 Italian war prisoners who could have been used to build roads. After the war, engineer officers who visited the island said that it would have taken two or three officers and minimal equipment to do the job. A road to Sfakia could have been constructed in six weeks with some road building equipment.

But instead of getting encouragement from Cairo, Brigadier Tidbury had his Cretan division yanked away and sent to Greece. He suggested that defenses against airborne troops be dug night and day until they were complete. His plan reached Cairo, and instead of approval he received orders for replacement. Thereafter, nothing was done. His successors were led to believe their only responsibility was to set up a headquarters that would be involved in the defense of Suda Bay. Nothing was said to them about the rest of the island.

However, there was some buildup. By the middle of April a battalion of the Second Black Watch had been sent to the coast at Iráklion. Two more battalions, the First Welch and the Second York and Lancashire, were stationed near Canea, with two antiaircraft units equipped with twenty-four searchlights, a field company of engineers, and a field ambulance unit. But air support was almost nonexistent, and the senior RAF officer on Crete was a flight lieutenant. The only aircraft on the island belonged to a motley outfit that was a squadron of the fleet air arm. But what a squadron! The aircraft were Brewster Buffaloes, Fulmars, and Gladiators, all of them obsolete. The Brewsters had never flown. They could not; Something was missing inside, from the moment of their shipment from America. The Gladiators and Fulmars would be prime targets for a Messerschmitt, and not much else.

Events moved so rapidly that when the British forces had to evacuate Greece in the last days of April, they arrived on a Crete which, far from being a redoubtable fortress, was still the sleepy little island that it had been before Churchill began talking about its defense.

But as the Greek campaign began immediately to go badly, the Middle East Joint Planning staff turned its attention to Crete in mid-April, and by April 21 had concluded that the defense of Crete would require three brigades of fresh troops and artillery which would concentrate on antiaircraft artillery, plus at least two squadrons of RAF fighter planes. The staff had already concluded that if the Germans conquered Greece, with their air power, the resupply of Crete during daylight hours would become impossible. But no one had paid any attention to that warning.

When General Wavell had that assessment, he passed the buck to London. He did not have the resources to fight the Germans in Libya, evacuate the troops from Greece, and resupply Tobruk, which was under siege. He also had to worry about Iraq, where the oil supply lay.

Prime Minister Churchill established the priorities. The battle of Libya was the most important. Then came the evacuation from Greece, and the resupply of Tobruk. No one expected an immediate attack on Crete, so that defense could come later, particularly, the prime minister believed, since all the planning and basic organization of defenses had been done since November. No one enlightened the prime minister about the true state of affairs on Crete. Even then General Wavell did not believe there was much danger for Crete. He underestimated Hitler's intention of crushing British power which might in any way interfere with the coming German effort in Russia. His plans included the protection of the Rumanian oil fields from RAF attack. As he wrote on April 24, even as the British forces and the Greek government were moving onto the island,

"It seems unlikely that the enemy will attempt a landing in force in Crete from the sea. An airborne landing is possible but not probable, since the landing force would be isolated without sea support." But he did anticipate heavy air attacks on the island, particularly since the Greek government was moving there.

On April 27, General Wilson arrived in Crete. Within a few hours, General Wavell had sent him a message. Could he hold the island with the troops who would be coming in from Greece? There could be no hope of much help from the RAF for some time.

Having gone through the battle of Greece, where the German air superiority was the major factor, General Wilson said that he expected the air superiority problem to be serious. Unless all three military services could put forth maximum effort, defending Crete, he said, would be extremely perilous. And he revealed that after six months of occupation, the British still knew virtually nothing about the island. They had not even reconnoitered the southern anchorages. He was being asked to defend something that he did not know much about, and neither did anyone else. In fact, the loss of Greece had indicated that a good case could be made for abandoning Crete immediately and moving everything to Egypt to concentrate the forces. The idea, in the back of Churchill's mind, of bombing the Ploesti oil fields, was now a long way in the future, because of Axis control of the air over the Mediterranean. The idea of using Crete as an advanced naval base did not have much appeal, given the Axis control of the skies over the island. Wavell and his generals already knew that with the circumstances that obtained, they could not hold the island. So why did they not just give it up? Because no one wanted to speak the unpleasant truth to Churchill, who remained optimistic and would brook no dissent at this point. And underlying all this was the mistaken impression of Churchill who believed that the basic defenses of Crete were in good order.

Having defeated the British in Greece, Hitler might have been willing to forego further action in the islands, except that the commander of the Luftwaffe, who had been responsible for the air campaigns in Greece and Yugoslavia, told him that the Ploesti oil fields were still within striking distance of the British bombers that could be stationed in Crete. General Halder, the army chief of staff, felt that to take Crete was to secure a power base in the eastern Mediterranean, and General Kurt Student of the Luftwaffe said that he could capture the island with airborne forces only. That meant Hitler did not have to worry about an amphibious landing, for which he was ill-prepared. Student made it look easy. Goering was convinced, and on April 21 took the matter to Hitler, who said he wanted to talk to Student. Hitler first thought the idea interesting but not practical. But Student's enthusiasm carried the day, for Hitler was always intrigued by the strange, and he had the feeling that the effect of an airborne success would bring a lightning-like reaction to the world. And when Halder and Goering heard, they thought this could be the stepping stone to success in Egypt. So Hitler was convinced, and on April 25 ordered Operation Mercury, which would be the capture of the island of Crete, to be accomplished by airborne troops and the planes of the Luftwaffe.

On April 26, General Wavell appointed General E. C. Weston to supervise the defense of Crete. On April 30, Wavell went to Crete to see for himself what was going on. He found that troops were still arriving in every sort of craft, most of them without parts of their equipment, some with virtually none of it. He called a meeting with General Wilson, General Weston, General Freyberg and others. First Wavell met privately with Wilson, and then Wavell asked General Freyberg to take command of the defense of Crete. Freyberg, the commander of the New Zealand Division, said it was his intention to get back to Egypt and reequip and strengthen his New Zealanders. Besides, his government would not stand for the continued splitting of the division so that he could take the bulk of it to Greece. But in the end he was persuaded to remain in Crete and assume command of the defenses. One of the last things that Wavell said to him was that he would have to do the best he could with virtually no air cover, against an expected blitz by the Germans. There simply were not enough aircraft in the Middle East for the job, and none could be brought from Britain in time to affect the outcome if the Germans moved as swiftly as everyone expected them to do.

CHAPTER 4

The Defenders

General Richard Freyberg, who commanded the defense of Crete, was a hero of World War I, who had swum two miles to a beach on Gallipoli Peninsula to plant decoy flares inside the Turkish lines, and had later won the Victoria Cross in France. Although he was fifty-two years old he could still swim farther than any man in his command, and he was known as "the soldiers' general" because of his concern for the men under him.

The first thing General Freyberg learned when he began looking around Crete was that he had no staff for the command, and that General Weston's staff was already moving back to Cairo that very day. Force headquarters was located in a quarry on the high ground between Suda Bay and Canea, along the neck of the Akrotiri peninsula. Within a matter of hours he was alone there except for Colonel Keith Stewart, his own chief of staff, who was the only man who had come to Crete with him. His trip to Crete had been expected to be only a brief visit to the two New Zealand brigades that had been evacuated here from Greece. Freyberg had wanted and expected to leave momentarily for Cairo to begin the rebuilding of his division when he had been shanghaied by General Wavell. And the reason that Wavell had chosen Freyberg, about whom he knew little, was that Prime Minister Churchill, a friend of Freyberg's from World War I, had suggested him for the defense.

So now, with the German attack expected almost momentarily, the new commander of Crete had to build a staff from scratch. He did so by selecting men from the ranks.

"I did not know the true state of disorganization until I went to Crete headquarters,'' he wrote Churchill. ''Although there was an officer's mess there were no staff offices for clerks, in fact there was no headquarters.'' He did not have a supply officer, or—and much more important—any trained intelligence officers. His own staff was now in Cairo and might as well be a million miles away. When General Wilson and the other commanders were considering the evacuation, there were at least four trained command staffs existent in Greece, but none of them had come to Crete.

Freyberg asked for the defense plan—and discovered that no one had drawn a plan. He began to understand why Wavell's Middle East headquarters in Cairo was known as ''The Muddle East.''

There were no accurate maps. He thought he could extend the road to the southern port of Sfakia. No one knew that the road ended on the top of a cliff hundreds of feet above the beach. He discovered that all the three airfields, the two harbors, and all the roads were on the north coast. And he had absolutely no information about the southern ports of Palaiokhóra and Tymbaki.

The situation of his new command was almost as bad. He did not know how many men he had. The best estimate was about 30,000 British empire troops, plus about 10,000 Greek and Cretan infantry men, only partly armed, and many with only a recruit's training. Some of the troops had left most of their equipment behind in Greece, or on vessels that went to Egypt. He discovered that his whole Sixth Brigade of New Zealanders was missing. It had been shipped to Crete on naval vessels, but after stopping briefly, the ships had sailed for Egypt, taking the men along. What he had left that he could rely on were his own men, about 9,000 of them, the Fourth and Fifth Infantry regiments, and the Maori Battalion. He had lost about a thousand men in Greece, killed or wounded or taken prisoner. He also had fewer than 10,000 Australians, ragtag survivors of the Sixth Australian Division. Brigadier G. A. Vasey, the senior Australian officer, counted five depleted infantry battalions and some artillery men. But about 5,000 of the Australians were unorganized, and Vasey considered them to be a menace to discipline, who had best be sent to Egypt as quickly as possible.

* * *

Then, too, there were the British, part of the Fourteenth Brigade, which had been stationed in Crete for several months. The First Welch Battalion was in the Canea area. The Second Black Watch was in Iráklion, with the Second Yorkshire and Lancashire Battalion, and in the Suda Bay area were 2,000 Royal Marines, plus about 400 Rangers and about 300 members of the Northumberland Hussars. There were also several thousand other British soldiers, most of them unarmed, with little organization and nothing to do. Some had stacked their small arms in a central storage dump, from which they apparently were never recovered, and had been abandoned in Greece. One soldier arrived with a greatcoat and blanket and not even a change of clothes, a brush, or a razor.

So General Freyberg discovered that he had drivers without vehicles, gunners without guns, and clerks without typewriters. Added to these misfits were the dregs of the British effort in Greece, deserters and malingerers who had been hastily shipped aboard any vessel at all, just to get them out of that country. Many of these people had already deserted again and taken to the hills. Others did nothing at all but complain about their rights and how they should have been shipped back to Cairo.

When the troops had arrived in Crete, they had been assigned to defensive positions in the order of their appearance, and so units were mixed and confused all over the island. The mutineers stayed in the hills all day and came down to the cafes at night to drink the local wine and fight, either among themselves or with the Cretans. To top it all, Freyberg was faced with an ill-matched assortment of refugees: Greeks, Cypriots, Palestinians, and Yugoslavs. They could be nothing but a burden.

As for the troops, the most serious problem was lack of equipment. There were virtually no trucks for transportation, no road building or earth moving equipment, and no tanks. The air force consisted of that odd squadron from the fleet air arm, plus a half dozen Hurricanes that had flown in from Greece.

On the afternoon of May 1, General Freyberg had a message from London, consisting of an evaluation of the military situation as of April 29. The Germans, it said, were collecting aircraft and would have about 300 transport planes. A division of airborne troops was already in the Balkans. The planners in London expected 3,000 German paratroops to attack in the first wave, and perhaps more if gliders were employed. There could be as many as two or three flights made by these transports each day from Greece and from Rhodes. Also, the Germans had plenty of shipping for tanks, so the scale of the invasion would be dependent on the German ability to evade the Royal Navy.

For air attack, the Germans were estimated to have about 300 bombers in the Balkans and some more in Rhodes. They had 60 twin-engined fighters and 270 single-engined fighters which would need extra fuel tanks to reach Crete and get back to their bases. They had 240 dive bombers.

When General Freyberg read this alarming news, he knew that if it was correct, his chances of withstanding a German assault were almost non-existent. He also knew that in London and the rest of the world, no one knew that Wavell and his Middle Eastern Headquarters had done nothing for the defense of Crete in all these months.

Freyberg sent a message to Cairo, saying that he felt he had to inform the New Zealand government of the true situation and that Wavell should reconsider the whole idea of trying to hold Crete. "The forces at my disposal are totally inadequate to meet the attack envisaged. Unless fighter aircraft are greatly increased and naval forces made available to deal with a sea-born attack I cannot hope to hold out with land forces alone which as a result of the campaign in Greece are now devoid of army artillery and have insufficient tools for digging and inadequate war reserves of equipment and ammunition."

He also sent a message to his government in Wellington saying that there was no evidence of either adequate air or sea power to repel the German invasion of Crete. He recommended that the New Zealand government press London either to supply the means to defend Crete or to evacuate the New Zealand troops from the island.

As for the troops, they knew nothing about the tensions in the various headquarters and in London. They had been evacuated from Greece to this lovely island, with its broad beaches and sunshine, and they were enjoying the respite. As far as they knew, soon they would be put aboard ship and taken to Egypt, where the war could begin again. Just now they were as if on holiday, and most of them were enjoying life thoroughly. The idea that the Germans might be preparing military attacks was far from their minds. Only four people on the whole island were aware of the truth: General Freyberg, his chief of staff, the clerk who typed the messages, and the cypher officer who coded them. Not even the general's brigadiers knew what was going on, and he did not burden them with the truth.

But he did write a special order of the day, hinting at what was to come:

"Today the British forces in Crete stand and face another threat, the possibility of invasion. The threat of a landing is not a new one. In England we faced it for nearly a year. If it comes here it will be delivered with all the accustomed air activity. We have in the last month learned a certain amount about the enemy air methods. If he attacks us here in Crete, the enemy will be meeting our troops on even terms and those of us who met his infantry in the last month ask for no better chance. We are to stand now and fight him back. Keep yourselves fit and be ready for immediate action. I am confident that the force at our disposal will be adequate to defeat any attack that may be delivered upon this island."

CHAPTER 5

They Called It "Colorado"

The stern messages that General Freyberg had sent to Cairo and Wellington soon provoked reaction. General Wavell sent a message to General John Dill, the Imperial chief of staff in London, indicating for the first time that there were serious problems about the defense of Crete. London read with astonishment that months after the orders had been given to prepare Crete, there were no roads in the south, no ports in the south, virtually no transportation on the island, no air defenses, and no modern aircraft. Wavell admitted now that the garrison was inadequate and that the island could not be supplied through the northern ports because of the danger of air attack. Until the southern ports could be made usable, supply was going to be an enormous problem. He also related the shortages of weapons and equipment and the unsatisfactory nature of most of the defending troops, who would prove to be a liability.

New Zealand prime minister, Peter Fraser, had just arrived in Cairo, *en route* to England, which could be an embarrassment. Prime Minister Churchill was quick to put the best face possible on the situation in Crete, in a way that could not possibly have been suggested by the military leaders in London. He indicated that Crete would be reinforced by the navy. He played down the danger from the air and the inadequacy of the British preparations, saying that matters would certainly be better in the Middle East in a month or so.

General Wavell tried to encourage General Freyberg. The London estimates, he said in his message, were exaggerated. He admitted that the air situation was grave, but promised full naval support, which Churchill had not, because in Churchill's list of priorities, the destruction of the German effort in North

Africa loomed even larger than Crete, and the Royal Navy could not do both jobs simultaneously and succeed in doing either very well.

The War Cabinet in London had said that Crete must be defended. That took care of Freyberg's request for a reassessment of the position. But Cairo would send artillery and other equipment.

General Freyberg was somewhat mollified by this message, because it at least indicated that Wavell understood the difficulties. Freyberg set about making the best possible use of his resources, and paid plenty of attention to the Greeks, whose land this was, after all. He met with the Greek army commander and with King George. He discovered that there were, as Wavell had indicated earlier, very few young men on the island. Most of them had gone to the armies that had been fighting on the Greek mainland. What he did have to work with was three garrison battalions with some training and eight battalions of recruits. The training program that Churchill had expected had totally failed to materialize. The whole population of Crete, including the convicts in the prisons, was prepared to fight, but the trouble was that very few of them knew how to do it.

Freyberg's staff wanted to discount the Cretans and the Greeks completely, but the general said they were wrong. In the three rocky hills of this island, the local people could be fearsome fighters, he was sure. The British must make every effort to supply them with weapons, and treat them as members of the defense. On May 3, Freyberg asked Cairo for 13,000 rifles and then another 20,000 to follow within a few days. He appointed liaison officers and training instructors to teach the Cretans the elements of infantry warfare. The weapons they had were a motley collection, no fewer than five types of rifles and machine guns that were antiques from World War I.

General Freyberg then organized 9,000 men into seven Greek regiments and a garrison battalion. The New Zealanders, with the support of two Greek battalions, would defend the ten-mile stretch of coast west of Canea. Another Greek battalion and a few New Zealanders would guard the harbor of Kastelli in Kisamos Bay, fifteen miles beyond Maleme. General Weston would defend the Suda Bay area, with the First Welch Battalion, the Marines, some Australians, some polyglot refugees, and a Greek regiment. What was left of the battalions of the Australian brigade—about half—joined the Greeks at

Georgeoupolis, fifteen miles west of Réthimnon. The Four
teenth British Infantry would defend Iráklion, with one Aus
tralian and three Greek battalions.

In all this, General Freyberg's greatest problems were lacl
of rifles to arm his troops, lack of ammunition for those rifle:
he had—some men had only three rounds—and lack of trans
portation. None of the units had enough trucks, and one New
Zealand brigade had only a single truck.

Besides, there was the problem of food supply for the
400,000 Cretans, 30,000 British soldiers, 15,000 Italian wa
prisoners and the Greeks and others who had escaped to thi
island. Crete was not self-sufficient in the best of times, and
now much had to be brought in by sea. The British would have
to keep those sea lanes open. Having disposed the troops
General Freyberg sat down to wait. What he was waiting fo
was not quite certain. Cairo thought it would be a seaborne
invasion, but one officer, who took a good look at the coastlin
in his sector, decided that the single beach where someon
might land successfully was so small that it required only a
single company for defense.

The soldiers waited happily. They swam in the sea an
sunbathed in the warm spring Cretan sun. More men con
tinued to arrive by caique from the Greek mainland. Almos
all of them expected to be leaving soon for Egypt. The though
that they would fight for their lives on Crete did not occu
to very many of the soldiers. And when the reconnaissance
planes came over, as they did with considerable frequency
they seemed small and lonely, and anything but offensive
droning away in the blue sky. The men went on picnics, an
spent their evenings in the cafes practicing their pidgin Greek
drinking wine, and talking. It was like a great extende
holiday, and except for the high command, no one wa
thinking of tomorrow.

As the planning and interchange of messages about defens
increased, Crete got a code name, Colorado. And in the re
quests and replies between Colorado and London and Colorad
and Cairo, a new optimism began to emerge. On May 5
General Freyberg cabled Churchill in London that he was no
in the least anxious about an airborne attack, but was worrie
about a combination of airborne and seaborne assault, if i
came before he got the promised artillery and supplies. Onc
he had those supplies and some transport, with a few extr

fighter aircraft, he felt it would be possible to hold Crete.

The possibility of seaborne invasion haunted General Freyberg. For defense against such an assault, he had to rely almost entirely on the Royal Navy. What he was trying to do in the early days of May was clean out the deadwood. He sent all the casualties who had come from Greece to Egypt by the first available shipping. On May 4, he asked for the removal of 14,000 troops who had no equipment and were already becoming a liability. In time of attack they would be an enormous problem. More than 9,000 of these men were shipped out to Egypt, but 5,000 remained, living in primitive conditions in the hills, with the wild actions of some of them jeopardizing relationships between the British and the Cretans. There also existed another insoluble problem: the presence of 15,000 Italian prisoners of war, who could not be moved, and who threatened to be a negative force under the conditions of battle.

By the end of the first week of May, another problem had begun to be important. The Germans were growing more aggressive in the air, and were attacking shipping and the docks of the Cretan harbors with increasing frequency. At first the attacks were not very successful. The cruiser *York*, which had been beached, still had her antiaircraft guns, and these popped away at the German planes, as did the antiaircraft batteries. By the middle of May, the attacks were occuring almost every hour, and some of them were sinking ships and damaging the docks. It was now true that Suda Bay could not be used in the daylight hours. Any ship that got in at night must get out by dawn or run the grave danger of being sunk. Then the Germans began to bomb even at night, which increased the danger. Actually, very few of the convoys got through to Crete, even in May. In three weeks, 27,000 tons of supply left Egypt for Crete, but only 3,000 tons arrived. By May 15, the Germans had established a complete daytime blockade.

General Freyberg kept sending lists of the supplies he needed. He got very few of them. Wavell promised him infantry tanks, but could not deliver rifles, and so when the actual fighting started, thousands of British and Greek soldiers had no weapons. A hundred field guns were sent from Egypt, but fewer than half of them arrived. Some of those that did were missing their sights or other instruments, and many were without ammunition. When the tanks arrived, they were found to have so many defects that they had actually been rejected by the Desert Army, so what use they were to be in Crete seemed hard to understand. What seemed to be happening was that the Middle East Command was sending anything it could conveniently get its hands on, just to be able to say supplies were being sent.

On paper the reports were impressive. On May 15, General Wavell sent a message to Prime Minister Churchill that indicated progress. Recent reinforcements, he said, included six heavy I tanks, sixteen light tanks, eight antiaircraft guns, seventeen field guns, and a battalion of men. He was preparing some other tanks and two battalions to land in the south as reserves. But when the tanks arrived at Suda Bay, the ship carrying them was almost immediately attacked by Stuka dive-bombers which had come in high and not been seen by the antiaircraft gunners. In a few minutes the ship was hit and was taking water. From *The Struggle for Crete*, here is the story of that particular important shipment from the officer who was in charge of delivering it:

"A few tanks in the upper hold were salvageable, but all the others and all the transport except the trucks on the deck were under water. Worst of all the wireless sets were a total loss. The harbor was being constantly bombed and we found great difficulty in persuading the Navy to give us steam to work the winches. After much thumping on the table in the office in Suda we persuaded them to bring a tug alongside to give us steam. Stripped to the waist we performed the unaccustomed role of dockers to unload tanks onto a lighter on the other side of the wreck. It was a terrifying job, working in the bowel of the ship up to our knees in water, at a time when the harbor was being heavily bombed. Every bomb, however far away sent concussion waves through the sea to crash against the hull."

Those tanks that were salvaged were moved out to battle stations west of Canea on May 18.

And as the Germans continued to build their air power and increase the attacks on Crete, there was not even much talk any more about British air reinforcement. The air force at Crete by this time had been reduced to three Hurricane fighters and three Gladiators.

Some useful supplies were arriving. With the arrival of a shipload, barbed wire began to spring up everywhere. Some guns came in, although they were almost invariably old and worn ones, not any of the modern guns that had recently arrived in North Africa.

More useful than the supplies was the intelligence that came to Crete in May. British intelligence outdid itself in Greece after the surrender, and kept sending in reports that indicated the intentions and the capabilities of the Germans. As suspected on Crete, the attack was to begin with an airborne assault by paratroops. The indication in May was that 5,000 paratroops would be involved, and their first effort would be to seize one of the airfields. After that was done, more troops and supplies would be brought in by plane. So the British effort must be to stop the Germans from getting the airfields at Iráklion, Réthimnon, or Maleme.

Despite this good intelligence, General Freyberg continued to be more concerned about the danger of landing from the sea than from the air. Each of his three major sectors of defenses in the north, where the attack would certainly come, contained an airfield and a port. The instructions were that a third of the troops were to be deployed around the airfields, with the remainder held back for reserve, either to counterattack the German parachutists, or to move to the defense of the ports if the invasion came that way.

The British defenses were well concealed. The men dug deep, narrow slit trenches around the trunks of the olive trees. These were sheltered from air observation, and because they were surrounded by roots, they were very strong, and would withstand anything but a direct hit from a bomb or shell. The antiaircraft guns were sited around the harbors and around the airfields. At Maleme, for example, the four coastal defense guns were controlled from Royal Marine headquarters, and the antiaircraft defenses from the Gun Operations Room. Ten Bofors gun installations guarded the airfield, but since their range was only about 800 yards, they were placed very near the runways, in full view of the attacking enemy planes.

By May 19, nearly 15,000 troops remained in the Suda Bay area, but the figures were misleading. Five thousand of these troops were totally useless, without arms, and General Freyberg was waiting for the ships that he had ordered three weeks earlier to come and take them to Egypt. Only about 3,000 of the men were properly equipped to fight.

A few rifles had begun to arrive from Egypt. There were still far from enough to go around, but the defenders made the best use they could of the material that came in.

General Weston placed his marines and odd lots of troops in defense of the docks of the Suda area. He put some of his troops among the olive trees between Canea and Suda. The Greeks had two battalions near the village of Periviola. King George of Greece arrived at that village with his government on May 19.

In the western sector of defense, the center was Maleme. There 7,700 New Zealand troops waited along the coast between the Tavronitis River and the Kladiso River. Reorganized into three brigades, these troops represented two-thirds of the original New Zealand division. They were under the command of Brigadier E. Puttick. The total strength here amounted to about 12,000 men. This included 3,500 Greeks who had no weapons, but they did have some artillery, about thirty guns of various sorts, and when the tanks were salvaged from the wrecked ships in Suda harbor, ten of the light tanks and two heavy tanks arrived here and were put out at the airfield in prepared shelters.

Brigadier Puttick had a difficult area to defend. West of Canea lay fields of grapes and barley, and then the plain broke into rolling hills and a broad valley that moved inland diagonally five miles southwest of Galatas, a valley crisscrossed by patches of cultivated fields and olive groves. Three miles from Canea stood the local prison, a white building in the middle of a circle of open ground. A mile beyond lay Lake Aghya.

The coastal road lay west over Canea Bridge, crossing the Kladiso River half a mile above the sea. A mile past the river lay the Seventh General Hospital on a flat hill, the ground around marked with red crosses. Two villages, Platanias and Modhion, hovered on the high ground. The road then became enclosed in walls of bamboo trees. Ten miles from Canea, it led into a scattering of houses and an olive oil factory on the right, and a group of small barns. This was Maleme, which included the large village of Pirgos. At the end of Pirgos was a small church and cemetery and beyond them, the airfield, with a single runway less than half a mile long, and the Tavronitis River. Leaving the airfield, the road wound around to the port of Kastelli, crossing the river on a substantial bridge. Beyond the river clumps of bamboo stood over the thick brush. But between the road and the shore the land was flat, and

Puttick saw that it was ideal for parachutists. Puttick sensed that this would be a fighting ground.

Brigadier Puttick's basic problem was that he had too much ground to cover, and General Freyberg kept impressing on him the need to guard against invasion from the sea more than from the air. He knew that the airfield was going to be a prime target of the Germans, but he could not give it priority over the port. So his troops were stretched very thinly across this large area. The Fifth Brigade guarded the airfield and the coast as far east as Platanias. This brigade was under the command of Brigadier James Hargest, another soldier from World War I. His defense line ran east and west from Platanias to the Tavronitis River, and he was to give especial care to the defense of the Maleme airfield. But at the same time, he must also be aware of the danger of attack from the sea.

This Fifth Brigade was a strong unit, as the defenses went, well trained in England by General Freyberg himself, strengthened now by a detachment of 364 engineers armed as infantry and two platoons of machine gunners, to give a total of 2,800 men. This unit had been reequipped, but was still short of grenades and mortars. The Brigade had seven French and Italian 75 mm guns and two 3.7-inch howitzers.

The defense of the airfield was entrusted to Lieutenant Colonel L. W. Andrew, with the Twenty-second Battalion, which was isolated, with headquarters five miles away, and the Twenty-third Battalion, stationed a full two miles away. The runway itself was hidden by a shoulder of the hills and by the thick bamboo that closed in on the road as it passed through the village. Even in clear daylight nothing could be seen of the runway from the main position of the Twenty-third, under the command of Lieutenant Colonel D. F. Leckie.

The rest of the brigade was spread out along the coast to the east. Brigade headquarters and the Maori Battalion were at Platanias, the engineers were next to them, and the Twenty-first Battalion was centered on Kondomari.

Lieutenant Colonel Andrew's problem with the Maleme airfield was that the distance from the runway to the sea was less than a mile. If visibility became impaired, it would be impossible to command the airfield from the hills around it. So he dug in one company on the perimeter of the field and placed another above the bridge of the river, while the remaining units occupied the village itself, to the south. To do all this he had 620 officers and men.

The most important elevation was what was known as Hill 107, located south of the airfield and not clearly visible from the position of the Twenty-third Battalion. The hill was about 350 feet high, red soil and clumps of scrub brush. Its face west of the river was covered by olive trees. This position was to control Maleme. Here Andrew put his command post and sited his two platoons of heavy machine guns to fire into the space beyond the river. His two tanks were dug in below the command post. The ten Bofors mounts stood nakedly on the edge of the airfield. Quartered on the east bank of the river, above the bridge, were about 350 officers and men of the RAF who had decided they did not want to learn to be infantry men. Although offered a course in instruction, they sat in their quarters and played cards and waited to be sent to Egypt. Lieutenant Colonel Andrew made the best use he could of the handful of RAF planes that remained. He investigated his defenses by persuading pilots to fly over and tell him what they saw. As a result, he improved his camouflage and his defenses. He had only one wireless set and his telephone lines were on top of the ground, leading to his companies, because there were no heavy tools to dig them in.

The Fourth Brigade stood west of Canea bridge, and also served as Force Reserve. The Tenth Brigade, which had been formed on Crete, was based on Galatas. This brigade was commanded by Brigadier H. K. Kippenberger. The center of the brigade's power lay in the composite battalion of 750 men, mostly gunners without guns who had been converted to infantry, and truck drivers without trucks. The trouble was that they were almost wholly untrained in infantry tactics. Besides this he had 190 men of the divisional cavalry without horses, and a platoon and a half of machine guns. He also had a battery of three Italian 75 mm guns which had arrived without sights, and with little ammunition. His two Greek regiments were virtually unarmed. He had no wireless sets, few digging tools and only one truck.

He placed his composite battalion along the hills from the sea to screen Galatas from the west. This should protect against any landing by the Germans on the flat ground near the prison, but it could only protect against German troops getting out of the valley. There was really nothing to stop them from landing there, since his troops were so widely dispersed. His Greeks, who had only three rounds of ammunition per man, covered the direct approach from the prison valley to Canea and Suda, at a point where the Alikianou-Canea road passed through a gap in the hills. North of Lake Aghya he put the 190 men of the cavalry. Across the road were the rest of his Greeks, about 900 in strength, but the brigadier had absolutely no confidence in them or their leader, so he put Major Clifford Wilson, one of his bright young officers, in charge.

If there was trouble, there was only one battalion in reserve. But the biggest problem of all was that if anything went wrong there was almost no communication except by field telephones, and no one expected these to last long. As for radios, there were not enough to supply one for each battalion.

In the Réthimnon sector, the enemy might try a landing at Georgeoupolis on Almiros Bay, twenty miles east of Suda or at Réthimnon itself, ten miles farther down the coast. Five miles beyond the town was a landing strip.

Brigadier G. A. Vasey had the Nineteenth Australian Brigade, two Greek regiments, and a battalion of Cretan police. In all, there were nearly 7,000 men with fourteen field guns and two infantry tanks. Vasey sent two of the Australian battalions, with most of the Greeks and eight of the guns and the two tanks, to guard the landing strip at Réthimnon. This unit was commanded by Lieutenant Colonel Ian Campbell.

The defense of Iráklion was a simpler matter than the others, because the port and the airfield were both within a perimeter five miles in depth. Brigadier B. H. Chappell had the Fourteenth Brigade, three regular British battalions, and a battalion of Australian infantry, plus three regiments of Greeks and some mixed groups of men, including some from the RAF. The total force here came to more than 8,000 men. They had twenty-nine field guns, six light tanks, and two infantry tanks. And on May 16 they were reinforced by the Second Leicester Battalion.

But if the defense of Iráklion seemed strong, it had to be, for this was the key point of Crete. The airport and harbor were the best on the island and at its center. If the Germans captured Iráklion, they had Crete in their pocket.

By May 18, General Freyberg was confident that everything

that could be done about the defense had been done on Crete. There were still serious shortages, the worst being in rifles and ammunition, but there was nothing that could be done about that locally. If Cairo could not send the supplies, they would have to try to do without. Now they waited, and by this time the euphoria was gone. With the disposition of the troops, the soldiers knew that they were soon going to be fighting the Germans.

Precisely when, no one knew. But in the second week of May, the German air attacks stepped up. On May 13, just after dawn, a large group of Messerschmitt fighters swept across the island in groups of five, and attacked the airfield of Maleme for an hour. That was indicative of things soon to come.

After all the defenses had been put together, one great question remained. What about the airfields? Of what use could they possibly be?

On April 22, it was estimated that a squadron of Hurricane fighters with constant replacement might protect Suda Bay. But the air marshalls of the Middle East were not inclined to expend their aircraft on Crete, and by May 5 had decided that it would endanger the British position in the western desert to send aircraft to defend Crete.

During the early days after the evacuation, there were a number of Hurricane fighters operating from Crete, remnants of the air force that had fought in Greece, and ten planes from North Africa. These pilots fought valiantly, as on May 13, when thirty Me-109s attacked the Maleme airfield. Sergeant Ripshjer, Sergeant Reynish, and Squadron Leader Howell each got into his Hurricane and began moving to the runway. As the German cannon crackled along the field, they managed to get off the ground. Half a dozen Messerschmitts flew directly down the airstrip as Squadron Leader Howell took off. Another wave of Me-109s skimmed along the beach looking for game. There were so many out there that no one could count them. The squadron leader was passed by two Germans as he gathered speed; they were going so fast that they slipped by and left him unscathed. He got into the air and headed for the protection of the hills.

Sergeant Reynish put his plane into a vertical bank with three Me-109s trying to turn inside him. Then he was on the tail of one of them, and it turned on its back, went out of control, and crashed in the hills. At this point twelve German planes were pursuing Sergeant Reynish, and he and they disappeared over the hills. Three hours later Squadron Leader Howell returned to the Maleme field. Reynish was rescued from the sea. Between them they had shot down six Messerschmitts.

The next day a Hurricane replacement arrived in the middle of an air raid, and the pilot, who must have been out of fuel, prepared to land although the field was under attack. He did not make it and dived into the sea.

It was very soon apparent to everyone that the number of Hurricanes steadily diminished and that they would soon all be gone. On May 17, the only three Hurricanes that could still fly were sent back to Cairo.

And what of the airfields, then? It was apparent that they would be of no use in the air defense of Crete, because there was no air defense and could not be any.

Each of the airfields, intact, posed itself as a prize for the enemy. Then why were they not destroyed, to prevent the Germans from making a successful landing? General Student counted on the seizure of one of those fields. If they had been made unusable he had no equipment with which to restore them, and the German invasion would most certainly have failed. At Maleme the staff captain of the Fifth Brigade had prepared to destroy the runway. He had mines set aside for that purpose. But they were never laid. General Freyberg was issued orders not to destroy the airfields, and these orders were approved by the British chiefs of staff. What could they have been thinking of?

After the fact they came up with a ridiculous self-serving memo that indicated how difficult it would have been to destroy the runways. That is true only if the destruction would have to be made in a few hours, and even then it was not true, given the mines that they had at Maleme and must have had at the other fields as well. If the plans had been made in early May, when it was already certain that the fields would be of no use in defense (because the RAF would not be there to use them) then destruction could have been done by men with picks and shovels alone. The tarmac could have been ruined and the surface made so uneven that it would take major earth-moving techniques to rebuild. But this was not done. Apparently it was not even contemplated until very late in the game. The whole showed a total incomprehension in London of the facts of warfare in the Middle East. But why had not Wavell and his staff come to the proper conclusion? The answer has to be that Wavell was really not very much concerned about Crete, except as a liability he had to deal with. By this time he was so deeply mired in Churchill's disfavor that nothing he could do would be viewed without suspicion. In the matter of Crete, in which the prime minister had his own decided views and his own local commander, Wavell must have felt that the less he did, the better off he would be.

As for Freyberg, he was under two mistaken impressions that colored all his views. First, he felt that the major danger from the Germans came from the sea, not the air. And second, he believed that the Germans could and would crash land their troops carrier planes wherever they wanted, without reference to the airfields. Thus, to him the airfields were not a major danger, and when the war cabinet and the chiefs of staff decided that they were to be retained, for some imaginary assistance that would spring up overnight, General Freyberg did not offer any objections. So the explosives sat in the airfield arsenals, and were never used for the one purpose that they might have served, to block the German reinforcement of their original airborne landings, and thus frustrate the German effort to take Crete.

By the middle of May, very few soldiers on Crete were still talking about the wonderful holiday they were enjoying. Several thousand who still expected to be evacuated because they had no duties or will or weapons with which to fight, wasted the time away, waiting purposelessly. Among the defenders, the feeling of tension began to mount. There were no more parties in the village squares and market places. The few soldiers who appeared in the streets wore arms and helmets and went about their business briskly. The ports were busy at night as the ships brought in more materials from Egypt, and everyone knew the vessels had to get in, unload, and get out again before morning brought the Luftwaffe. The men worked all night in the ports. Fighter planes began to roar over the island almost everywhere, at any hour after dawn until any hour before dusk. Trucks used the roads gingerly, the drivers having helpers along to look for air attack. Two doctors were killed while swimming near the hospital. One afternoon, hundreds of planes were over Suda, hitting the defenses the pilots could see, and on their way back they strafed the trenches on the Akrotiri peninsula. As long as the men stayed in their slit tenches they were safe, but if they got out, they became the targets of the planes, and several were killed.

A newspaper began to appear in May, produced by several of the New Zealand soldiers. It was called the *Crete News*, and it had the latest rumors and the latest information about the war in other sectors. The few wireless sets that existed were tuned to the BBC and to radio Berlin to listen to Lord Haw Haw, the British traitor. Every night he referred to the coming battle for Crete, which he called "the island of doomed men."

The bombing increased every day, and in Britain the expectation was very great for the defense of Crete. Some of the important members of the government seemed to regard it as something like a football match, and Churchill himself talked about the wonderful opportunity to thrash the Germans. Crete would be defended to the death, Churchill told the House of Commons. All over the world, the newspapers were full of talk about the coming fight for Crete. There seemed to be very real understanding outside the command of the island itself as to the very small chance the defenders would have of achieving a victory.

CHAPTER 6

The German Plan

When General Kurt Student convinced Marshal Goering and Hitler that the Luftwaffe could carry out an invasion of Crete without the support of ships and seaborne forces, he bit off a big chunk of assignment. The Germans had used airborne troops before in Holland and against the Belgian forts with great success, but the airborne forces had always been backed up by armor, artillery, and regular infantry, all of which arrived in short order. This time the airborne forces were undertaking to do the job by themselves with the air support of the planes of the Luftwaffe, plus a Mountain Division and an armored division. The major assault would be made from the air, with supplementary forces to follow with such vessels as could be gotten together. How this was to be done, and when, was left very fuzzy in the first planning. The airborne assault was the major effort.

General Alexander Loehr, the commander of Air Fleet IV, was responsible for *Einsatz Kreta* (Operation Crete). The first attack would be made by parachute and glider troops of the Seventh Air Landing Division, part of General Student's XI Air Corps. The airborne troops would establish bridgeheads, and then troop-carrying aircraft would land with the Fifteenth Mountain Division and the Fifth Armored Division's vehicles. It was estimated that 22,750 men would be involved within three or four days.

The air transport would be provided by 500 troop carrier Junkers JU 52s from XI Air Corps and seventy or eighty gliders. The reconnaissance and bombing of the island would be left to General Wolfram von Richthofen's VIII Air Corps, which numbered some 280 bombers, 150 Stuka dive bombers,

200 Messerschmitt 190s and twin-engined ME 220s, and various reconnaissance planes. The total air strength available was 1,330 planes, a far larger figure than estimated by British intelligence. The big problem for the Germans was time. The new date set for the postponed invasion of Russia was June 22, and that had to be firm so the Russian campaign could be carried out before the onset of the Russian winter. Thus, the Crete operation must be completed by that time.

In this race against time, General Student had to supply the airfields from which the Luftwaffe would operate, and this meant bringing in aviation fuel in barrels, and transporting them mostly by sea, since the roads in the Balkans, indifferent at best, had been chewed up in the Greek and Yugoslav campaigns. Student was an experienced officer, having been involved with the German air force since the days of the first World War, and then joining the Luftwaffe as soon as it was formed. He had been inspector of parachute troops before he was given command of the paratroops. His subordinates found him more of a dreamer than an operator. One of his subordinates, General Meindl, said of him that he had big ideas but no conception of the details necessary in carrying them out. But others were more charitable, and gave Student credit for inspiring the troops with his cool bearing and apparent confidence.

The decision to attack Crete was made on April 25 as the British troops were still pouring into the island. The paratroops were still in their barracks in Germany, but they were rounded up and put on trains to Prague, sent through Hungary and Bulgaria, and then trucked down into Greece.

Each parachute battalion was divided into four companies of about 110 men each. The Storm Battalions, the glider troops, were slightly larger than the Parachute Battalions. The paratroops carried Schmeisser machine pistols and a few grenades. Their supplies were to be dropped along with them in canisters, which contained light field guns, machine guns, rifles, mortars, grenades, and ammunition for the weapons. The Storm Battalions carried their own rifles, machine guns, and other weapons, and so they could get into action the moment their gliders landed. The technique that had been used in Holland was to bring the gliders in first, and then for the Storm Battalions to protect the parachutists, who were half paralyzed when they dropped and had to have time to find the canisters, open them, and sort out the weaponry.

In Crete, the German plan was to land the glider troops and the paratroops around the airfields and to capture one airfield as swiftly as possible. Then, the heavy aircraft could come in bearing more troops and heavy weapons. The British had feared all along that the Germans intended to crash land their transports on the beaches or in the fields of Crete. That was not the case; no such German intention existed.

General Student had proposed first that the airborne troops make six simultaneous landings along the north coast. General Loehr suggested that they concentrate their effort in the Maleme-Suda area. Student objected to this plan because he felt that the British could then concentrate their defense. And he entirely overestimated the really nonexistent strength of the RAF. He wanted to hit all the airfields at once. This brought up the problem of the Greek air facilities. They would not support such an extended operation, if the Germans could mount it. So Marshal Goering suggested that the airborne forces arrive in two sections on the first day.

The invasion would be preceded by heavy bombing and fighter sweeps that were supposed to so effectively destroy the morale of the British defenders that when the airborne troops arrived they would be thoroughly confused and unable to organize resistance.

The Maleme-Suda sector would be hit first at 8:15 in the morning. Most of the gliders would land here. The parachutists would then drop around the three airfields and in the southwest near Alikianou. The Germans had no shortage of radios: Every glider platoon of thirty men would have two radio transmitters, and radio communications and recognition signals had been worked out carefully to help the air force and ground troops work together.

The planes would fly back to their Greek bases and take off again at 2 P.M. with the second strike, which would start dropping on Iráklion and Réthimnon about 4 P.M. The 9,000 parachutists of the division would all take part, plus 600 men of the Storm Battalions. As soon as the airfields were captured, the planes would return with the first 5,000 men of the Fifth Mountain Division. Meanwhile the troops and supplies that would come by sea would be off the coast of Maleme on the afternoon of the first day. Another convoy would arrive east of Iráklion on the second day. Each convoy would carry an infantry battalion of mountain troops, heavy weapons, and supplies. And 2,000 parachute troops for whom there was no space on the aircraft would also come in by sea.

The sea invasion, which caused so much concern among the British, was not considered very important by the Germans, except to maintain communications and establish services of supply for the troops once the invasion was completed. They did not expect that the Italian minesweepers which would come in would arrive until the third day of operations. The whole German plan depended on the success of the airborne landings, and Student envisaged the capture of the British headquarters by the end of the first day.

The British attempts at camouflaging and concealing their defense activity had been successful in one way. The German pilots who flew the reconnaissance missions came back to report that the island seemed lifeless. They saw no concentrations of infantry and little shipping. So the Germans came to the conclusion that most of the troops were being evacuated by night, and that all that remained on the island was about a division, in addition to the Greek remnants who had escaped to Crete. So while British intelligence about the Germans was reasonably accurate, German intelligence about the British was woefully inaccurate. General Halder, the chief of staff of the German army, put it succinctly: nothing they knew about Crete was definite.

In fact, many of the impressions the Germans had about Crete were completely wrong. They believed that the wide valley southwest of Canea was a high plateau. They did not know what sort of country surrounded the three airfields. And without significant geographical information, they were mounting the largest air landing in history, and depending on the airborne troops without the almost immediate support of motorized infantry and panzers.

General Student also would have liked to have total control of the operation, but he did not get it. Control rested with General Loehr, and Student did not even have control of the VIII Air Corps, for which he would have to depend for air support. On the first day of the operation, he was committing almost all of his forces, including the 2,000 men who would come in by sea bringing the heavy equipment. He was holding only 400 parachute troops in reserve against some trouble. This meant that if the air landings did not produce the almost immediate capture of an airfield, the whole operation would face disaster. The British believed that the Germans had several airborne divisions and parachute divisions, but the fact was that there was only the single parachute division, and even in Germany there were no reserves. Everything was being committed in this one great blow, and if trouble came, the only reinforcements could come in by sea. And by the time they arrived, it might be so late that they too would face disaster.

In the third week of May, the Germans were nearly ready to stage their invasion. General Student called a conference at the Hotel Grand Bretagne in Athens. The commanders of all the paratroop regiments and battalions were assembled to receive their orders. A large map of Crete was hung on the wall. General Student explained the plan of attack which Student had worked out with Goering and General Loehr. When he had finished speaking, the corps intelligence officer sketched the enemy's situation as it was known to the Germans. All that remained on the island, he said, were the remnants of two or three Greek divisions and a British force of about a division, consisting of dominion troops under the command of General Freyberg. Some of the population would be sympathetic to the Germans' attack. (The British already knew this. They had picked up several Cretan spies for the Germans, including one orange vendor who had marched the through the camps collecting the numbers and dispositions of the British units for the Germans.) There was also a "fifth column" which was prepared to fight alongside the Germans and which would make itself known to the paratroopers by the code words "Major Bock."

Meanwhile, the German troops were relaxing beside the airfields of southern Greece, waiting. The members of the Storm Regiment had been given passes to go into Athens, where they saw the Fifth Mountain troops marching down to the dock at Piraeus.

At noon on May 19, the paratroopers learned that their objective was to be Crete. They were told when they would attack the next day and where: at the three airfields of Maleme, Réthimnon, and Iráklion, They were also told that they would then be reinforced by troops from the air and from the sea.

That evening, the Germans sent even more bombers and fighter planes than usual over Crete, and the British sensed that the attack could not be very far off.

CHAPTER 7

The First Day—
The Airborne Assault

For several days after the middle of May, General Freyberg had been receiving messages from Cairo suggesting that the attack on Crete might not come off at all, and that the Germans might be preparing to attack Cyprus. This rumor was largely a product of the imaginations of the Muddle East staff, who were muddling again because Prime Minister Churchill had just ordered them to prepare an attack on the Vichy French in Syria and Lebanon, which they did not want to carry out.

Prime Minister Churchill was hoping for a victory in Crete. It was clear that he still did not understand that the lack of preparation and the lack of air cover made such a victory virtually impossible. Now the failure of the defenders to destroy the airfields made a defeat almost certain. General Freyberg had convinced himself, however, that he had a chance of holding Crete, and he was going to do his best.

The latest word, issued to the battalion commanders on May 16, was that the attack could come at any time from the seventeenth to the nineteenth. The British expected an airborne force of 25,000 men or more and a seaborne force of 10,000 men. First would come air assault by bombers and fighters, and then the landing of troop carrier planes, followed by the landing of the paratroops. The seaborne troops would be escorted by the Italian navy. The objectives of the airborne forces would be Maleme, Canea, Réthimnon and the Aghya valley. When General Freyberg had this information, he replied that he felt he could deal with the airborne invasion, and that the seaborne invasion was the one that troubled him. So once again, the British showed their basic lack of appreciation of the airborne and air power and their continued traditional thinking that kept them from the obvious course of destroying the airfields and frustrating the airborne invasion before it began.

That night of May 19, the invasion had not yet come, but the German air assault did begin. Two German airmen, rescued from the sea after their plane crashed off Crete, told a Cretan fisherman that the invasion would begin at dawn. It only added to the apprehension of the British command.

The British soldiers had spent the day cheerfully without much concern for the next day. The German planes had swept over them at treetop level, but so artfully were the defenses created that the Germans saw virtually nothing and hit virtually nothing with their strafing and bombardment. At Maleme six men were injured by the attacks. Virtually all of the artillery remained intact.

By seven that night, as darkness was falling, the last of the German aircraft left the area, and the villages became very quiet. The night sounds of clattering dishes, glasses, and song were heard in the streets of the towns, and there was music and the sound of radios to entertain. Soldiers and civilians ate their evening meals, drank tea and wine, and enjoyed the beautiful weather. And then Crete slept.

At three o'clock on the morning of May 20, the glider troops and parachute troops of the German air landing division were awakened in the darkness and ordered to prepare for the day's adventure. As the false dawn came, they were on the airfields and gathering beside the aircraft that would take them to Crete.

Just after 6:30 that morning, the JU 52s began to take off, some of them pulling gliders. Soon they assembled over Athens and then headed south.

The defenders of Crete were arising in the chill of the morning and preparing for the day that might bring excitement. At 7 A.M., General Freyberg knew that the assault was coming, with word of groups attacking the coast between Suda and Maleme. The bombers and fighters were doing their job.

Then the defenders heard another sound, the droning of many engines, coming down from the north. On Hill 107, above the Maleme airfield, the defenders crouched in their slit trenches. It seemed that the German attack this morning was more severe than usual, but so far no one had been hit. They were not to move or take any action until they were sure the invasion from the air had really come. The first formations to begin bombing were JU 88s. As they heard the noise of the engines the men below began to duck into the slit trenches. When the whistling of the bombs began, they threw themselves flat and listened to the racket of the explosions, coming in groups of twelve, with shocks that reverberated across the hills and could be felt in the trenches. Soon the whole area of the airfield was covered with choking dust, and the men could not see more than five yards in any direction. More bombs kept whistling down, so they kept their heads down. Bombs struck on the hill and covered some of the trenches with inches of dirt. The turbulence was enormous.

The Germans had hoped that this bombardment would have shock value far greater than the destruction caused, and they seemed to be right. The Bofors guns on the perimeter went silent one by one as their exposed crews were hit and killed or wounded. The last gun kept firing for a long time, until attacked almost simultaneously by Stukas and Me-109s, which silenced it as well as the others.

Suddenly the bombing stopped, and the silence was almost too much for the men to bear. Blue sky began to show through the swirling dust. It was eight o'clock. Then the men saw the first of the gliders. They seemed huge and menacing. They came gracefully, swooping down like hawks from the mountains, in spiral turns down to their landing places. One dropped at the edge of the shore onto a rock and crumpled. Another smashed against the bridge on the river. Others landed on the river bed, and the British defenders could see figures running from the gliders to disappear into the bushes. The enemy had landed. The invasion had begun.

The German bombing and strafing had produced the desired effect, at least at Maleme. Squadron Leader Howell, with no more Hurricanes to fly, was fighting as an infantryman, and he occupied a slit trench on Hill 107. When the bombing ended, he felt numb and dazed. His head was ringing, and he could not think clearly. His men seemed to be as badly shaken as he was.

Very few of the German aircraft and gliders had been hit by the antiaircraft guns; only seven transport planes of 500 were knocked down. But after the bombing ceased and the gliders began to come in, the machine gunners on the hills around the airfields began to wake up. They started firing, and some of the gliders crumbled and crashed. Several gliders that had been hard hit landed, but no one came out. All the men inside had been killed by machine-gun fire. Some crashed into the rocks, and the men inside came tumbling out to be met by more machine-gun fire. In the RAF camp, one aircraftman stood shocked beside his tent when a glider burst through the bushes and crashed, one wing up against the hillside. He emptied his rifle into the open doorway, blocking it with bodies before running up the bank.

Within half an hour, the sixty gliders that had landed on Crete were down, at Maleme, in the Prison valley, and on the Akrotiri peninsula. Many of the soldiers who had ridden in them were dead before the fighting really began.

But now the parachutists began to descend. As the blossoming parachutes came drifting down, many of the defenders were still transfixed in shock, doing nothing but watching. The Germans came down shouting to each other. The defenders stared at the green, red, yellow, and white parachutes. Then they came to life and began to fire. Several hundred parachutists fell within the areas of the New Zealand Twenty-third Battalion, two miles east of the Maleme airfield. Lieutenant Colonel Leckie killed five parachutists coming down inside his command post in a ravine near the road. His adjutant shot two more. Every ten or twelve yards a parachutist landed, and was shot before he got out of his harness.

On the airfield itself, the machine gunners fired until their gun barrels burned out, and then retreated to a prepared position. But not all of the parachutists were killed. Soon the survivors were out of their parachutes, and throwing grenades and firing their Schmeisser machine pistols. At Galatas, Brigadier Kippenberger's command post in the village square was overrun by gliders. He escaped up the hillside and shot a German in the yard of a house. He moved his command post to the headquarters of the composite battalion a mile northeast of Galatas. The landings in this area were light, but by 10 A.M. he had the word that 55 parachutists had been killed or captured, while southeast of the village 155 had been killed by the Nineteenth Battalion, which had taken nine prisoners. Farther south, the Germans had dropped in force across the Prison valley in the midst of the Sixth Greek Battalion, whose men had only three rifle rounds apiece. These were soon gone and the Greeks were dispersed. The New Zealanders were surprised, because ammunition for the Greeks had arrived some days earlier but had never been distributed below the command level. That day, the Greek colonel was shot by the New Zealanders, who claimed he was throwing grenades at them. Before noon, the Germans had overrun the headquarters of Colonel Kippenberger and the Galatas heights. They were moving up through the olive groves on both sides of the road.

In the Fourth New Zealand Brigade area, the Eighteenth Battalion was commanded by Lieutenant Colonel J. R. Gray. Three of his companies were facing west on the coast road a mile from Galatas. At about 9 A.M. they saw their first parachutists dropping out of the transport planes a few hundred feet in the air, the figures falling, then jerking, and the parachutes opening. Most of these men were falling in the area of the Seventh General Hospital. Lieutenant Colonel Gray rallied his men and moved up the ridge in the direction of the parachute drop. Parachutists were descending from the last planes, and many of them had already reached the ground. He and his men stopped and shot those still in the air, then headed up the ridge toward the others. He saw a parachute hanging from a tree and shot him. He and his men shot many others, and captured a few, most of whom were wounded. But the parachutists by this time had occupied the Hospital peninsula, seized a field ambulance, and captured several hundred hospital patients. The Germans shot the doctor in charge of the ambulance, who died in a slit trench. But they did not massacre the patients. They collected those who could walk, about 300, and marched them up the slope to Galatas, where they expected to find Germans ensconced. But instead, they met more New Zealanders, who began to fire on them. They later claimed the Germans were using the patients as a protective screen. By late afternoon, all the Germans had been killed or captured, and the patients who had not been killed in the fighting were released.

As had been foreseen by General Freyberg, the big problem for the British was weapons. The gunners did not have rifles, but they begged them, borrowed them, and stole them, and when the Germans came down dead, they took their rifles and fought with them as long as the ammunition held out. But sometimes they had no chance. East of Galatas a troop of Royal Artillery was placed with four field guns to fire down onto the Prison valley or the beaches. But these gunners had no personal weapons at all, and when parachutists dropped on them, they were overrun in a few minutes. They managed to spike three of their guns, but one was saved by the Germans and used later in the battle.

The 3.7-inch heavy antiaircraft guns at Sternes were defended by men who had somehow gotten hold of their weapons. The other half of this battery was close to Canea and had been issued rifles and other weapons, among the last to be passed out before the invasion. A glider landed nearby, and the ten men of the German unit got out and soon disarmed the British gunners, lined them up, and shot them. Then the executioners were surrounded by Royal Marines who saw what they had done and killed them. Those who tried to escape were burned to death when the marines set fire to the cornfield in which they were hiding. There had been 180 gunners in the German unit. At the end of the slaughter seven survived, and none of them among those who had shot the British soldiers.

News of this episode soon spread through the defense, and the British suddenly realized that this would be a fight to the death, without quarter, The realization of the bloody truth of the encounters was on them now. Most of their anger was reserved for London and the high command that had deprived them of the weapons with which to fight such an invasion.

It was worse than anyone had thought. British and Greek soldiers breaking into the warehouses at Canea, found rifles and ammunition that had never been distributed, plus Italian machine guns and ammunition.

In the field, the men began to search the bodies of the Germans, taking every weapon and all the ammunition of the dead paratroopers and glider soldiers. All along the coast it was the same. By noon the Luftwaffe was back to help the Germans, but in most areas the pilots hesitated to attack the men on the ground because it was hard to tell friend from foe. Had the German pilots known the real facts, it would not have been quite so hard. The British had been instructed to wear shorts, because the rumor had been passed that the Germans would come wearing British battle dress. It was not true; the Germans were in heavy woollen uniforms, far too heavy and uncomfortable for easy fighting. This was one of the few advantages the defenders had.

The assignment for capture of the airfield at Maleme had been given to the Storm Regiment, which consisted of three parachute battalions and 350 glider troops, somewhere between 2,000 and 2,500 men. Their commander decided that he would bring the gliders in to the perimeter of the airfield and the parachutists a mile or two away. Nine of the gliders, including the regimental command post, would come down on the river bed with the road bridge as their objective. More gliders would carry the headquarters staff and two companies of the first battalion, which meant about 250 men. One company would land at the mouth of the river, but the other would take Hill 107 and then attack the airfield.

The Second Battalion and the Fourth Battalion, about 600 men each, were to move along the coastal strip, west of the river. A small detachment would attack the village of Kastelli and the Third Battalion would take the coast road east of Pirgos. Thus the airfield would be attacked from three sides.

That was the German plan, but from the moment that the first glider hitland, the plan was in trouble. The Germans had no protection along the shore. From Hill 107, heavy machine gun fire poured down on the gliders as they came in, and as the German soldiers scrambled out of the gliders, bullets were puffing the sand around their feet. Only in the riverbed was there some shelter for them. The survivors of the first landing moved quickly to seize the RAF camp on the eastern bank, scattering airmen and driving them up the hill. They captured the bridge, but once across it, they were under the fire of the New Zealand C and D companies, and their commander and his executive officer were both killed.

The German assault on Hill 107 was a failure. Most of the gliders were shot to pieces as they hit the ridge, and the commander of this unit was severely wounded and most of his men killed. Those who escaped went to the west, and were rallied in the riverbed. But the Hill still stood and poured out fire.

The German paratroopers who landed west of the river in the bamboo and barley fields suffered least. Their heavy weapons and their motorcycles were mostly wrecked, but they had few casualties. They were puzzled, because there was no defense here, yet this was the area that had caused so much worry to General Freyberg because he did not have enough troops to defend it. The Germans had lucked into just the right place.

The German Third Battalion came down southeast of Pirgos, where the parachutists landed almost at the feet of the Twenty-second and Twenty-third battalions, which were ready for anything. Many of these parachutists were killed as they came down, and the bodies collapsed beneath their colored parachutes. Those who managed to land, came down inside the British perimeter, where they were dealt with swiftly and brutally before they could collect their weapons from their canisters. About 400 of the 600 paratroops of this battalion were killed in the first few minutes of the fighting. All the officers were killed or wounded. The survivors were men who had been dropped in error across the valley west and south of Pirgos, where there was no defense and nothing to defend. Little groups were able to establish positions there and wait for something to happen.

When Major General Meindl, the commander of the division, jumped in at 8:30 A.M. it was immediately apparent to him that the plan had failed. The gliders were to have come down and the troops to have established themselves around the airfield. It had all gone wrong with the Third Battalion on the eastern side of the airfield. What the Germans had to do now, and do in a hurry, was to capture the heights south of the airfield. And he would have to use the two parachute battalions that had dropped to the west, where they were relatively intact.

So Major General Meindl ordered up two companies of the Second Battalion to move on Hill 107 from the south. Down in the riverbed he had the survivors of the glider force, about a hundred of them, a company from the intact Second Battalion, and three companies of the Fourth Battalion. The major general knew by noon that something terrible had happened to his Third Battalion. That meant that he could expect a counterattack at any time. If he was going to capture the heights, he would have to do so without delay.

Before General Meindl could do anything about the attack, he was wounded, and then wounded again, the second time in the chest, a serious wound. He was carried to a field casualty center the Germans put up in the bamboo by the road, and there he remained conscious and in control of the regiment for several hours.

The British had their own problems. Brigadier Hargest at Platanias learned of five gliders landing on the Tavronitis river bed at 8:30. How he got the message so quickly would remain a mystery, because of the paucity of radios. Apparently it came by telephone, and apparently it came from the men on Hill 107 who had the clearest view of the fighting of any group. Lieutenant Colonel Andrew, who commanded the sector, had to guess at the strength of the German attack. He estimated that 650 paratroops had landed in his area. The truth was that

1,000 men had come down safely here west of the Tavronitis. This was the force that the British had to fear—intact, disciplined, and ready to fight. Lieutenant Colonel Andrew had sent three observers to watch from the heights in the west, but none of them ever returned. If they had only been able to get back, or if they had had any way of communicating, he might have been informed. But as it was, from the west of the airfield came no news at all.

By midday, the Germans were in serious trouble and suffering heavy casualties, although here and there they had their initial triumphs. Near the river mouth, the Germans cut off a platoon of the New Zealanders, twenty-two men under a lieutenant who had been assigned to guard a front 1,500 yards long on the edge of the airfield. They were armed with grenades they had manufactured from jam tins filled with concrete and gelignite. But they managed to hold off the Germans until nightfall, although cut off from north and south.

In the Maleme area the main British defense line held solidly, having fought off the glider troops in the beginning. The Germans had taken the RAF billet area and the bridge. Late that afternoon, the Germans began to approach the northwest perimeter of the airfield, but they were unable to gain a foothold there. The airfield remained a no-man's-land.

But the Germans were advancing doggedly where they could. Two companies in the south began to come up toward Hill 107. They reached the rear slopes of the hill about nightfall, but were so exhausted from a long day in the sun, with temperatures higher than 100° F that they could not think of mounting an attack.

Lieutenant Colonel Andrew did not know they were there. He had a radio, but part of the time it was out of commission. His telephone connection to brigade headquarters had been broken by the bombing that morning, and in the fighting was impossible to repair. He was also out of communication with D company on the western face of the hill and the headquarters company, which had been cut off by a group of German parachutists. He sent out runners, but none of them got through. What really worried Andrew that evening was that he was out of contact with his battalion. Heavy mortar fire from the Germans down in the RAF camp caused him to pull his headquarters several hundred yards back to the reverse slope of the hill. From here he could no longer see the runway of the airfield.

He sent up flares, a prearranged signal that called the Twenty-third Battalion to make a counterattack from its position on the edge of the airfield, toward Hill 107, thus attacking the Germans down in the riverbed. But the flares produced no results, so he was in touch with Brigadier Hargest by radio, repeating the request that the Twenty-third Battalion be sent to counterattack. The word he got back was that the battalion was busily engaged with paratroopers and could not launch an attack. Therefore Andrew decided that he had to launch a couterattack of his own to clear the Germans from the bridge area. He had little in reserve except the two salvaged tanks that had been his share of the extra defenses. He sent these and the survivors of a company which had been decimated in the fighting, one of the artillery officers who was with his command, and six of the artillerymen. The first tank, it was quickly discovered, had the wrong ammunition for its gun and thus could not fire. It lumbered forward and then stopped suddenly on the road. The second tank moved down below the bridge driving the Germans to cover, and firing rapidly until it got stuck in the riverbed among the big boulders. There it had to be abandoned. Without their tanks, the infantrymen and the artillerymen were caught in a hail of German fire from the front and the slopes on the left, and only a handful of them made it back to the hill.

Andrew soon learned from one of the survivors what had happened to the tanks, and that the two platoons on the perimeter down below had been overrun. He still had not heard from D Company and Headquarters Company, and he feared the worst. The Germans might even now be landing troop carrier planes on the captured airfield. But they were not, and that meant that some men still were fighting in those areas. Because he could not see the areas affected, Andrew came to believe that all his forward elements down by the river had been destroyed and the Germans were in control. He reported this to Brigadier Hargest, and also reported the fact that the Germans who had reached the bottom of the hill were now beginning to attack. Unless he could be reinforced, he said, he would have to undertake a limited withdrawal to prevent the Germans from getting behind him. Hargest could offer him nothing but the acquiescence in his withdrawal if it was necessary.

Adding to the difficulties of the defenders this evening was a new series of selected attacks by the Luftwaffe. Obviously, the Germans were making good use of their excellent radio communications, and from the riverbed they called on the Luftwaffe to make strikes on Hill 107, a point so eminent and so easily located by reference to the river, the airfield, and the bridge that the pilots could scarcely miss it. So in the dusk, the Luftwaffe was sending Me-109s to hit the hill.

It was 6 P.M. Andrew was preparing to withdraw when he had a new message from Brigadier Hargest. The brigade was sending two companies to support Hill 107, Hargest said. Expecting the support very soon, Andrew decided to hold out where he was.

At brigade headquarters, Brigadier Hargest was living in a fool's paradise, largely of his own making. The Twenty-third and Twenty-first battalions were both available and willing to go to Andrew's assistance, but they were never told what was happening on Hill 107. The Twenty-third had spent a relatively quiet day after destroying the German Third Parachute Battalion as it came down on them early in the morning. The losses of this battalion had been only seven men killed and thirty men wounded. Lieutenant Colonel Leckie had been told by Brigadier Hargest that there was no need for him to counterattack, and that he was to stay in his position.

The Twenty-first Battalion was holding the ridge lines and vineyards which lay north and south between the villages of Kondomariko and Xamoudhokhori. Initially it had dealt with some 70 paratroopers. After that assault was ended, the battalion sent a patrol down toward the Tavronitis River, but it ran into that strong German force down there and was stopped half a mile from Hill 107.

Lieutenant Colonel J. M. Allen, the battalion commander, did not know what was going on with the other battalions. His telephone lines had gone out during the Luftwaffe bombing attacks, and he had no radio. His only method of communication was by runner. Since he did not know what was going on, he elected not to follow up his patrol and go to the assistance of the Twenty-second Battalion on Hill 107. He did not really know how serious the situation was, or whether he might expect another bout with the parachutists dropping on him, so he remained quiescent. Brigadier Hargest was content with that, for he was completely misinformed about the German strength down by the river and on the far side. He believed it consisted of about 150 men, when actually there were more than 1000 German paratroopers concentrated there and preparing to attack the airfield.

As I. McD. G. Stewart says in the exhaustive *The Struggle for Crete,* what was surprising to him in his researches was that the messages that came in to the brigadier late in the afternoon of this first day of attack did not shake the confidence that he had that everything was under control. He told Lieutenant Colonel Andrew that he could not have any help from the Twenty-first or Twenty-third Battalions. Hargest had some misgivings, obviously, when he learned that Andrew planned to retreat, and promised him two companies. But the news that the tank attack had failed did not seem to impress him enough to cause him to revert to the original plan, which called for the Twenty-third to attack in support of the Twenty-second if necessary.

Andrew waited for the two promised companies. By 9 P.M. they had not arrived, so Andrew told Hargest by radio that he was going to have to withdraw as earlier stated. The brigadier gave no reaction. Author Stewart concluded for some reason, either the weakening signal of Andrew's radio, or his own presumption that the Twenty-second Battalion was threatened by only 150 troops, Hargest failed to understand the Andrew predicament. Nor did Hargest seem to appreciate the gloomy prospect that if the Twenty-second abandoned Hill 107, then it would have to be recaptured or the airfield would be lost.

On the night of May 20, the Twenty-second was fighting the Germans on its hill. The Twenty-first and Twenty-third Battalions were quiet. The entire Fifth Brigade, which could have gone to the assistance of Hill 107 with about 1,700 infantrymen, settled down for the night, its commander not knowing that by his inaction he was imperilling the entire British defense of Crete.

CHAPTER 8

The First Day—
Down in the Valley

The Germans had planned to drop most of their troops in the center force on the Canea-Suda area. The Second Parachute Regiment would attack Réthimnon, and by nightfall the Germans should have captured Canea, Suda, and Réthimnon. The command center would be seized and British organized resistance brought into confusion in the first few hours of the invasion. It should all be over in three days, and the mines cleared out of Suda Bay so that German and Italian vessels could use the port.

This task was given to Lieutenant General Suessmann, who was to land by glider with his headquarters near Lake Aghya. The 3,000 men of the Third Parachute Regiment and a Parachute Engineer Battalion would be accompanied by some small detachments with heavy weapons. Thirty gliders would bring in 270 airborne troops of the Storm Regiment, and most of these would attack the antiaircraft batteries around Suda. Fifteen gliders would attack the guns on the Akrotiri peninsula, and nine would attack the battery south of Canea. The Third Battalion would be dropped east of Galatas. The First and Second Battalions would drop near the prison, and the Engineer Battalion would drop north of Alikianou.

But on the flight to Crete the planes towing the gliders got separated, and when they arrived in the Suda area they were hit by heavier antiaircraft fire than expected. The gliders cast off their tows at 6,000 feet, and most of the pilots found it hard to identify their proposed landing spots. Four gliders were shot down by the British, and several others smashed on the rocks. The men who came out of the wrecks alive found themselves widely scattered. They also discovered that they were in the wrong places, and the guns had been moved by the British since the German plan was drawn. Their venture was a total failure. Of the 150 men, a third were killed and the rest either wounded and captured or taken prisoner.

The section that attacked the battery south of Canea got down all right. From this group, ten men in one glider were the ones who killed almost all the 180 artillerymen serving the heavy antiaircraft guns south of Canea. But the rest of this section milled about, and late in the day were ordered by radio to withdraw to the prison.

The Third Parachute Regiment's First Battalion dropped south of the prison and the Alikianou-Canea road, and at first had little opposition in this undefended sector. The men occupied the prison. One company reached the village of Perivolia, not far from the outskirts of Canea, where they were held up by Greek and British troops.

Much of the Second Battalion dropped on the north slope of the valley close to Galatas, in the olive groves. They encountered heavy fire from the ground as soon as they jumped and their parachutes opened, and many of the men were killed before they reached the ground. Those who came down near Galatas were nearly all killed very quickly. One company of Germans dropped a mile south of the town and moved ahead until they encountered a British company under Captain W. G. McDonagh. His men fought the Germans hard and killed many of them, including the German commander. But McDonagh was mortally wounded in this engagement and his men were forced back.

The German Third Battalion was scattered in its drop, spread over three miles between the Hospital peninsula and the foothills west of Perivolia. Most of this battalion's members were killed during the day.

At the southwest end of the Prison valley, the Engineer Battalion fell into the local brush, which happened to be thickly mingled with cactus. After the men picked themselves up, they encountered Greek troops and local Cretans who were even more prickly: they shot at the Germans with everything they had, from shotguns to muskets. The Eighth Greek Battalion was less than a thousand strong, but later the Germans were to claim that there were 4,000 of them. The Greeks were quick to pick up the German arms that came down from the sky and turn them against their owners. The Greeks fought valiantly, losing their commanding officer and most of the staff during the day, but they killed many Germans. Next day a New Zealander in the area counted a hundred German bodies in one small area near the road, about a mile from the village. When night fell, the Greeks had been driven up to the ridges, but they hung on there and held the village of Alikianou.

Lieutenant Farran, the officer who had been in charge of salvaging the tanks from the bombed-out ships from Egypt, had saved three of the tanks for his own unit, which was posted near the Galatas turn in the road. When the parachutists began dropping, Farran did not wait for orders. He drove up the road through Galatas, passing through New Zealanders who gave him the thumbs-up signal. Then he was out in the olive groves, looking for Germans, who were very elusive, particularly when they saw the tank. But the tank lost a track. He had to abandon it and make for safety on foot.

In Galatas, a British officer who was attached to one of the headquarters had come to this area on an official visit, and conveniently forgot to return to headquarters. He organized the Greeks of the battered Sixth Greek Regiment, found them arms, and took over their leadership in the Galatas area. They were sandwiched in between a New Zealand company on their right and the Nineteenth Battalion on their left. That afternoon they counterattacked the Germans in Galatas, driving them out of the village.

All the way through this operation, the Germans suffered from their lack of knowledge of the terrain, and errors in planning made because aerial photographs can give only limited information. In the area near Lake Aghya, as noted, the gliders were to land and set up a headquarters. But no one knew that the place they had chosen to land the gliders was full of the stumps of old grapevines, which were invisible from the air, but which tore the bottoms out of the gliders as they landed, killing and injuring most of the passengers. General Suessmann, who had planned to put his headquarters here, did not arrive. His glider broke up and crashed in the Mediterranean on the way to Crete, and there were no survivors. Command of the division and of the group in the center now passed to Colonel Richard Heidrich, commander of the Third Parachute Rifle Regiment. When he got down to the ground, he discovered the awful truth: They were not on a plateau at all, but in a valley, and he must fight his way upward to capture the heights on the left flank.

The morning was spent in planning and finding the lay of the land. By mid-afternoon he had collected a force of about 400 men and began to move toward Galatas to attack. The attack did not succeed. Just beyond the prison they came to a little eminence known to the defenders as Pink Hill. Here the unit called the Petrol Company was dug in, and they fought back when the Germans came up. The Germans had no time or opportunity to find the canisters with their heavy weapons and had to attack only with their Schmeisser machine pistols. The British, with rifles and Bren guns mowed them down, showing fine fire discipline by waiting until the Germans had come within easy range and then opening fire. The fire was fast and heavy, and the Germans suffered 50 percent casualties before they could pull back with their wounded.

As evening approached, the Germans tried again, bringing in troops from the southern flank to help. This time the Germans took Pink Hill, and the Petrol Company retreated. The Germans also took another rise in the cemetery, but the village of Galatas remained in British and Greek hands.

The British still commanded the situation in Prison valley, but the Germans were moving. If the British counterattacked at this point, they might retrieve all the lost ground and finish off the threat here. Brigadier Kippenberger, who was in charge of this sector of the defense, applied to headquarters for a counterattack at this point. But nothing happened, and Kippenberger began to fear that he would have to abandon Galatas.

He did not know what had happened to the Eighth Greeks, and as far as he could tell, the Sixth Greeks had simply disappeared. The only unit under his command in which he had any confidence was the Nineteenth Battalion of New Zealanders. Meanwhile, his units were feeling German pressure on the left, and two companies had been forced to retreat. They had suffered sixty casualties, including four officers.

He was afraid that the Germans were clearing a landing field in the prison area, and that is one reason he was so interested in securing a counterattack. If there was no counterattack, he proposed to move back along the Maleme coast road. In any event, he did not believe he could hold the line against an attack the next day.

But when Brigadier Puttick received this message from Kippenberger, he refused to commit the Fourth Brigade to such an enterprise. This was his divisional reserve. But because of Kippenberger's erroneous statement that the Germans were building a landing strip near the prison, Puttick did order the dispatch of one battalion to the area to clear out the Germans and then take over the defense where the Sixth Greeks were supposed to have been.

The figures now coming in to headquarters about the landings were slightly more realistic than the early ones. The Nineteenth Battalion reported that evening that about 1,200 Germans had landed in Prison valley. The truth was that a considerably greater number, about 1,500, had parachuted. Of these, some 500 had been killed, but that still left a force of more than 1,000 men down by the river.

The British attack was launched with only about two companies participating. It forced the Germans to leave Pink Hill, but did not do much else. It was too late in the day for anyone to see very much of what was happening. The Germans, hearing the sound of the three tanks that the British had decided to employ here, became very worried, recalled the battalion that had reached Perivolia, and ordered the Engineer Battalion to close up from its position down in Alikianou.

The Germans that evening were seriously concerned about their whole enterprise. They had been given a great deal of misinformation, ranging from the geographical features of the island to the attitude of the Cretans, which Admiral Canaris's military intelligence organization had indicated would be very favorable, but which was anything but. Division headquarters had ordered reconnaissance of that area on the "high plateau" considered suitable for the landing of transports. This, too, had proved to be a complete illusion, and the "high plateau" was, instead, a river valley. That night, the German commander of the large force in the valley worried that his remnants of a thousand men would not be sufficient to withstand the counterattack he fully expected in the morning from Galatas.

For Brigadier Puttick that night, it was time to try to put together the facts of the day. He had the Fourth Brigade almost intact, and now the decision had to be made as to how they could be used to best advantage.

What would happen tomorrow? The British expected more parachute troops to come, and they looked over their shoulders at the sea, waiting for the sea invasion that General Freyberg anticipated. And what of Iráklion and Réthimnon? Apparently, they had scarcely seen any enemy except for the Luftwaffe attacks.

Several senior officers had asked for counterattack in the Maleme sector during the first day, but Brigadier Puttick would not commit the troops. Thus, he lost the advantage of that period during which the Luftwaffe was loath to take any action, because the pilots could not decide from the air which were British and which were German figures on the ground below. But by nightfall, the Germans were giving the Luftwaffe position fixes, and tomorrow might be a different story.

From Brigadier Hargest came a most optimistic report about the situation around Maleme airfield. Hargest still did not understand the threat to Hill 107 and the inability of the Twenty-second Battalion to hold without assistance. But at ten o'clock that night, Brigadier Hargest was still issuing optimistic reports about the Maleme area. It was not until midnight that the truth began to emerge, with information that the Twenty-second Battalion was beset by Germans who had arrived at the bottom of its hill, and that it might not be able to hold the hill the next day. Even that came in as whispers and rumor, and not as hard fact.

As the British were puzzling about what to do the next day with their reserve brigade, which was their striking force, the Germans were planning their own moves. After the day of confusion, the paratroopers were in touch with the Luftwaffe, and the next day they could expect air support for their activities. At the outset of the British defense planning, General Freyberg had made the point that the airborne troops must be subjected to counterattack at the first moment, to put them off balance and wipe them out before they could get properly organized. But here in Prison valley, the Germans had been allowed to remain unmolested for a full day, first because no one knew how many there were, and second because of the reluctance of the British high command to commit its force. So the opportunity of May 20 in the Maleme area had been thrown away. That night, even as the generals considered the situation, three New Zealand battalions were available to make a strong counterattack, supported by a platoon of machine guns and a group of light tanks. But no one said anything to them about the next day. And the British in Iráklion and the rest of the island waited for the other shoe to drop.

CHAPTER 9

Iráklion

Iráklion, the port on the eastern end of the north shore of Crete, boasted a modern harbor and a modern airfield, and was thus prized by the Germans. But their initial attack on the western end of the island was occasioned because the ancient city of Canea was the capital.

The town itself, which was protected by the three Greek battalions and the York and Lancashire Battalion, was ancient and walled, but a radar tower overlooked the town, and the airfield that lay close to the beach from the high hills of the east. By the day of the German attack, May 20, 1941, the British Fourteenth Brigade had been built up to 14,000 troops, two heavy tanks, and half a dozen light tanks.

The airfield was three miles from town, and between town and airport the road divided a meadow known as Buttercup Field from the Greek barracks, a modern multistoried yellow building. Brigade headquarters was located north of the road and west of Buttercup Field, and the Leicester Battalion, which was the brigade's reserve, was quartered south of headquarters. The Second Black Watch Battalion occupied the perimeter of the airfield, whose runways crossed. A mile southwest of them were two other eminences, small conical hills that the Australians referred to as "Charlies" because of their breastlike shape. The Australian Battalion occupied these eminences. The defense area was small: Both the airfield and the harbor could be surrounded by a perimeter four miles long and two miles wide. A mile inland was another eminence, Apex Hill, and four miles south of the harbor lay the ruins of the ancient Greek city of Knossos.

Brigadier B. H. Chappell commanded the defenses of

Iráklion. His orders were to defend against invasion from air or sea, and also to prepare to support the Australians who were defending Réthimnon farther west along the north shore. "Everything must be done," said General Freyberg, "to insure that communications with us are maintained."

Freyberg's orders for the defense stipulated that the troops would remain concealed until the German bombing and strafing attacks ended. When the paratroops and gliders began to land, they were to be attacked immediately, with the Leicester reserve battalion assigned to the attack on the airfield, supported by the tanks. The antiaircraft guns would reserve their efforts for the main attack.

The commander of the German forces in the Iráklion attack was Colonel Brauer, of the First Parachute Regiment of the Air Landing Division. He had his regiment and a battalion from the Second Regiment, plus two odd companies, a total of 2,600 men. One battalion was assigned to capture the airfield and another the harbor. The two other battalions would cover the approaches from east and west to prevent reinforcements from arriving. On the second day, the sea force would reach the coast and deliver a battalion of mountain troops and several hundred parachute troops for whom there had not been enough aircraft. The sea force would also bring up 88-mm guns and other heavy weapons.

For two days before the attack, the Luftwaffe did its best to knock out the defenses of Iráklion. Hundreds of bombers and fighters screamed across the town and the airfield, tempting the Bofors gunners to reveal themselves as the Germans dropped their bombs and strafed. But the gunners held their fire, the troops retreated into their slit trenches and concealed positions, and few men were hurt.

The morning of May 20 dawned bright and sunny, as usual. A flight of Messerschmitts circled about the harbor and the airfield looking for targets to attack and finding nothing much. Then they left, and no more came. The British defenders returned to training exercises. They had no inkling of the attack that was occurring to the west. Obviously, the communications between Iráklion and the defense headquarters in the west had already broken down. At noon, as the German JU 52 transports were returning to their Greek airfields to follow Marshal Goering's instructions and pick up the second load of paratroopers, the colonel in command of the Leicester Regiment was going to the only hotel in Iráklion that boasted a bathtub, to spend an hour relaxing. While he was there, the Luftwaffe attacked again, this time in a specific softening-up process, aiming at the Black Watch positions on the airfield, at what they thought were the antiaircraft guns around the town, and the dummy aircraft parked on the airfield aprons. They dropped many bombs, and the Messerschmitts came in to strafe again. They were gone before the colonel had gotten back from town. As several officers who had watched the German air show attested, it was spectacular, but it was also not very effective. Few casualties resulted. The antiaircraft installations were intact, and the defenses were basically unaffected.

After that attack, there was silence. The Germans were having difficulties with their two-stage air attack. The landing of the Luftwaffe attacking aircraft and the troop carriers returning from Crete had raised clouds of dust on the Greek airfields. The Greek underground, which had already sprung up, was sabotaging the telephone system, which the Germans were using for communications for this operation. As a consequence, the troop carriers planes were delayed at every step, from refuelling, to loading their paratroop passengers, to takeoff. When they did begin taking off it was in the wrong order, which confused the battle plan for the landings, and when they got to Crete they found that the confusion had deprived them of the fighter air support.

The British troops saw the flashes of light on the JU 52s as they came in to the coast late that afternoon. Then the planes crossed the coastline and suddenly the air above the Iráklion area was full of parachutes, and the anti-aircraft guns which had been so silent for so long began to fire. A JU 52 was hit and crashed before it could drop its paratroopers and the air drops were confused, with men dropping into the teeth of the British enemy. One paratrooper came down on top of a British company headquarters, to be greeted as he landed by half a dozen infantrymen, with bayonets fixed: One British soldier heard the German scream.

For the soldiers below, it was like target shooting as the Germans drifted down. They would pick a target, fire, and then, as they saw the figure go limp, pick another and fire again. Those paratroopers who were so unlucky as to land in trees or in the telephone wires were riddled. Some paratroopers fired their Schnmeissers at the British as they came down. One, at least, came down with his hands up, and then began throwing hand grenades.

Some came down in the turnip fields and began a frantic chase of their weapons canisters. Others fell in the vineyards or the cornfields, and tried to rally.

Because of the German confusion, the airdrop lasted nearly two hours. Six hundred of the paratroops did not get airlifted at all, because of the shortage of aircraft. Two thousand of them arrived, but hundreds were killed before they hit the ground. The one thing that was obvious about it all was that the German intelligence agencies had completely misinformed the command about the strength and character of the British defenses. They had expected to jump on a relatively easy target. Instead they jumped into fury.

The German Second Battalion had been assigned the capture of Iráklion airfield. The companies on the east side that fell into the Black Watch perimeter were decimated, with only one officer and sixty men surviving the first few minutes after the drop. The troops that dropped on the west were destroyed in about twenty minutes by the withering fire from the Australians and from the mixed group of troops near brigade headquarters. The light tanks came out and cleaned up the area until virtually none of these Germans survived. Five men of two companies managed to get to the coast and swim to a point where they could join another band of survivors. Within the first hour, the Second Battalion had lost twelve officers and three hundred men killed, and eight officers and one hundred men wounded.

The two German parachute battalions that landed west and south of Iráklion met the Greeks outside the city as well as a company of Yorkshire and Lancashire riflemen who were on the west wall of the town. The Germans who survived the landings got to the moat around the wall, and no farther.

Some of the Germans managed to get inside the city gates, and that night they reached the water of the harbor. But there they encountered the "friendly" Cretans, and the night was punctured by the sound of shots and flashes of gunfire and the sound of running feet. The Germans inside the city were like sacrificial lambs.

East of the city at his command post, Colonel Brauer soon realized that he had lost his Second Battalion, and that the whole attack plan had miscarried, largely because of the miscalculations of intelligence about the strength and willingness to fight of the British enemy. All he could be sure about at this point was his own headquarters and the First Battalion, which had been assigned to the east side of the airfield. Of this battalion, only one company had arived on schedule, and the other three had been scattered as they fell some distance away. It was midnight before the Germans in platoon strength reached the defense line of the Black Watch. Brauer also learned that the First Battalion of the Second Paratroop Regiment, which was part of his force, had made a safe drop west of the town and met no serious opposition.

The full extent of the disaster was still not known at the command post. The Germans had lost half their Iráklion force, and a whole battalion had been left behind in Greece. This aspect could have been foreseen. The Luftwaffe should have expected casualties among the troop carriers and planned accordingly. The confusion threatened the success of the whole operation that first night. With so little information to go on, Colonel Brauer could only stick to his orders, and they called for him to continue the attacks at dawn. He sent the orders to his battalion commanders by radio that night, knowing that the orders to the First Battalion were now meaningless.

The British defenders at Iráklion had reason to be encouraged that evening. The main defenses had been cleared of the enemy. Small parties still lurked in the town, but they were being hunted down by the Cretans and the Greeks. The airfield was secure, and a thousand German bodies had been counted inside the perimeter. The officers now praised their noncoms, who had taken the initiative and launched their counterattacks as soon as they had sight of the paratroops. Half the German paratroopers had been killed within a few minutes of leaving their aircraft. There had been no time to collect guns and automatic weapons. And the British casualties were very low. One Australian company had killed ninety of the enemy with a casualty list of three dead.

As darkness fell, the British could see that the enemy was still with them, Colonel Brauer's men were sending up flares to make contact with one another. In the town the sound of gunfire continued as the hunt for the Germans went on. Brigadier Chappell had a major problem: He had absolutely no communication with the east, so he did not know what was happening at Canea and Suda. Nor did he know what to expect in the morning. Another parachute drop? The invasion from the sea that the high command had been talking about for so long?

So a night of waiting began on both sides.

CHAPTER 10

The Réthimnon Airstrip

General Student had selected Colonel Sturm, a veteran of the parachute actions in Holland and at Corinth in Greece, for that parachute attack on the Réthimnon airfield. A force of about 1,500 parachute troops had been assigned to him for the task. A third of them were to land to the east of the airfield and then move to capture it. A larger group would land three miles to the west to capture the town. The rest of the troops would belong to the headquarters company which would be with Colonel Sturm.

From the intelligence reports, the capture of Réthimnon seemed a simple enough task. There were not any signs of powerful resistance, and the job should be completed within a few hours. Before the first day was over, Colonel Sturm should be able to lead his men to join up with the group at Suda.

The British defense at Réthimnon was in the charge of Lieutenant Colonel Ian Campbell, who had previously been serving in the western desert. He had two Australian battalions of 600 men each, a small artillery force and two platoons of machine guns, 800 Cretan police, and 2,500 Greeks, many of whom had no arms at all. The biggest problem was lack of ammunition for the artillery, with only five rounds each for the antitank rifles, and eighty 3-inch shells for the four mortars. The machine guns were short of ammunition, and so were the riflemen.

Here the airfield lay south of the road, five hundred yards from the beach and five miles east of town. A steep plateau surrounded the eastern end of the airfield. This was called Hill A. From this point, a narrow ridge moved off at right angles three miles to the west, as far as the village of Platanes. The ridge was split by two gullies, or wadis, Wadi Pigi, a mile to the west, and Wadi Bardia, cutting to the sea along the face of Hill A. Between them the ridge line was called Hill D. Hill B was close to the village of Platanes, and Hill C was a mile from Réthimnon. Several villages dotted the coastline, some with churches and other substantial buildings. A road ran behind the coastal ridge through a narrow valley to join the hamlets of Pigi and Adhele to the coast road near Platanes.

Campbell had put his men along the foothills, at points from which they would be able to stay under cover while sweeping the field with gunfire. He had six old French and Italian field guns and a heavy machine gun platoon dug in on the forward slope, with a good view of the landing strip to the north, east, and west. The guns were hidden in the trees.

One battalion, two more field guns, and a machine gun platoon were on Hill B with the left flank south of Platanes. All this was commanded by Major R. L. Sandover. The Cretan police guarded the town of Réthimnon and the Greeks filled in the gaps between the Australians and remained with the tanks hidden behind the ridge.

As with all of the defense of Crete, the communications between units were primitive and could not be expected to last long. The only recourse after the telephone lines were cut was the use of runners. There was a single radio transmitter.

All during the previous weeks, the British garrison here had remained invisible to the Germans. By May 16, the Germans had only been able to identify a single defense position, and when photographs of that place were found in a crashed German observation plane, the position was abandoned in favor of another.

Because of the shortage of roads, it was difficult to move around the area in the daylight hours without being spotted by the Messerschmitts that were almost constantly overhead. Campbell did so by motorcycle, moving in short jumps.

The first sight of the enemy on invasion day was a look at a group of JU 52s flying low along the coast in the direction of Canea. That was all the defenders saw and all they knew, but they assumed that the Germans had begun their attack in the west.

The first contact with the enemy came at about four o'clock in the afternoon when twenty Me-109s and light bombers attacked the area. But as usual, they did not find the defenders, but dropped their bombs mostly harmlessly, on the hillsides.

The landings began at four-fifteen that afternoon. The troop-carrying planes came as expected from the north, crossed the coast to the east, and then flew down the beach, dropping their paratroops from a height of 400 feet. The antiaircraft guns shot at them and downed several. At the end of an hour, the British had counted more than 160 planes.

From the German point of view the landings were not a success. In the first place, they took too long. And then many of the paratroopers were dropped in rocky country and were injured as they landed. Only two companies fell into their planned drop zones close to the eastern edge of the airfield. They were immediately attacked by the Australians from Hill A. All the officers of one German company were killed. The survivors could not find their weapons containers in the rocks. It was two hours before they began to show some semblance of order, and were able to join up with the eastern companies.

The Germans attacked Hill A, and they soon captured all the field guns and killed most of the machine gunners. By nine o'clock that night, they held all but a few bits of the northern slope. The rest of the Australian company had been forced back to the southern section of the hill.

Farther west, the British fared better. Many of the parachutists were shot in their harnesses as they landed in the vineyards before the British battalion. One planeload of paratroopers was wiped out completely before a man touched the ground. Most of the paratroopers who jumped here were captured or killed, and only a few escaped to join the Germans at the foot of Hill A.

The Germans who fared best were those who landed farther down the coast. They moved towards Perivolia and soon came up against the Cretan police.

At about 5:15 P.M. Lieutenant Colonel Campbell decided to use his tanks to clear the Germans from Hill A. They moved down the Wadi Pigi, but again, as at Maleme, the tanks did not do well. One got stuck in a gully and the crew was captured. The second fell into another wadi eight feet deep and its crew was killed.

Campbell then saw that he would have to recapture Hill A, and he set about planning for that move as the darkness fell over the area. He realized that the heights were the key to the defense, and asked for help from Canea by radio. He waited then for six hours, only to receive the disappointing reply that no help could be expected. So he was on his own in the defense of Réthimnon. If he waited, the Germans might bring in more troops, which would make the situation worse. At the least, they would be better organized by the followeing morning. So Lieutenant Colonel Campbell began collecting his forces. He would make a dawn attack.

CHAPTER 11

The Battle Scene

On the morning of May 20, General Freyberg and members of his staff stood on the hill above his headquarters on the Akrotiri peninsula and watched as the Luftwaffe attacked again, as it had so many times before. But this day it was different. Soon they could hear the throbbing of many more engines, and it was not long before the transports and the gliders began to come in view. Half a dozen gliders sailed over the general's head on their way to Prison valley. The first planes carrying paratroops headed for the airfield at Maleme, circled counterclockwise, dropped to an altitude of 500 feet or less, and then spewed forth their parachutists.

The general went down the hill to send a message to Middle East headquarters. The attack had begun, he told them. He could not even estimate the forces involved.

Two hours later, he was no better informed. All he could really attest to at this stage was what he could see. The assault had barely begun, and already his communications were in tatters. Most of the telephone lines from the units around Canea and Maleme had been destroyed by the Luftwaffe bombing or cut by the parachutists after they got down. Some units were already reduced to using runners for communication, and were so busily involved with the enemy that they had little time to think about messages to keep the high command informed. Reports and rumors were so intermingled as they came in that he could hardly tell one from the other.

The first real news began to arrive at headquarters at about nine-thirty that morning. General Freyberg learned that the parachutists had dropped in the area of the Twenty-third Battalion and the Twenty-second Battalion. The Twenty-third was having no difficulty.

Then General Freyberg had disquieting news from Brigadier Puttick. It began with a report that troop carrier planes were thought to be landing three miles south of Maleme and in the riverbed west of the airfield. The rumor gained authority, and the second message said that a large number of troop carriers had landed under the mountains southwest of the reservoir. Then came a third message, even more authoritative. The Germans were clearing the area around the prison for the landing of troop carriers.

All these reports originated with Brigadier Puttick, and all were untrue. Whatever landed in those areas was either a glider or a crashing transport plane and the Germans were not clearing the prison area. But General Freyberg believed the reports because he was conditioned to believe. So embedded in the British consciousness was the myth of the power of the Luftwaffe that no one in the British establishment involved with Crete questioned the assumption that the Germans could afford to expend transport planes on one-way flights to attack the enemy. The truth was, of course, that the German air capability was strained and overextended in this whole operation. Proof of that is the failure of one whole battalion to be airlifted on the first day of battle, and the dispatch of two thousand paratroops by ship because the Luftwaffe did not have the aircraft to even think of bringing them by air.

But General Freyberg had fully expected the Germans to find places to land their aircraft outside the airfields, and this led to his continuing basic error in defense strategy because he did not place very much importance in the denial of the airfields to the Germans. Since neither he nor any of the other British leaders involved understood airborne operations, they did not know that General Student from the beginning had been placing his whole hope for success on the quick capture of an airfield, so that transport planes could bring in the heavy weapons which would tip the scale in favor of the Germans. Without weapons and supply within a few hours, the German effort was bound to fail. Student knew it; Freyberg did not. In a sense this was the essence of the entire battle.

The rumors continued to pour in to Freyberg's headquarters, and the facts did not. After the Germans seized the hospital and began trying to march their walking wounded prisoners along the road, the rumor came that the parachutists were moving swiftly along the road to Canea. It was afternoon before the general learned that it was not true, that the Germans had been stopped, and the hospital had been reoccupied by the British.

Next came a rumor that the king of Greece and his ministers had been captured. Parachutists and gliders had been seen heading for the area where he was living. The truth was that The king had already left the area for a more sheltered spot in the mountains.

Brigadier Puttick continued to be a font of misinformation. His next wrong report concerned the enemy. The parachute landing had been made by 1,500 men, said Puttick, and from the evidence of a captured officer, they were very disturbed by the reception they got. Part of that statement was true; the Germans *were* disturbed by their high losses, and by the fact they had been misinformed by German intelligence about the nature and strength of the British defenses. But Puttick's misstatement about the number of Germans involved had to be dependent on wishful thinking, compounded by bad intelligence questioning and appraisal of statements from captives. More than 6,000 Germans had landed.

By midafternoon, General Freyberg's information about enemy strength had not improved much, and he was still operating on the basis of misinformation. The rumor persisted as fact that the Germans were building a landing strip by the prison. Freyberg indicated in a message to Cairo that he was planning a counterattack on that area of the valley northeast of Alikianou.

But even more important than the misinformation was the fact that General Freyberg had relinquished control of operations to Brigadier Puttick without ever saying as much. The Fourth Brigade was the island's task force, and it was inherent in the defense that the brigade would be sent into action to counterattack. On this day, as the Germans threatened the Maleme airfield, the logical move would have been to rush the brigade to wipe them out. But Puttick did not have the imagination to take such action or the faith in his subordinates to believe Lieutenant Colonel Andrew's contention that he was in real trouble on Hill 107 that evening of the first day. And so, as the battle raged on the hillside, and the Germans were winning it, the force that could have annihilated them was left sitting idly in its encampment all day long.

It was not long after the parachutes began to fall at Iráklion and Réthimnon that General Freyberg learned of this new set of attacks. When he was asked for help that evening by Lieutenant Colonel Campbell he did not know what to do. So he did nothing for six hours, and then told Campbell there would be no help. There actually could have been help available in the form of two Australian battalions near Georgeoupolis who had not come under any attack, but Freyberg was so uncertain of the enemy and his future actions, that he refused to budge them. But that night he was given the whole German operation plan of the Third Parachute Regiment, which was attacking in the Maleme area, where the situation was dangerous, if not critical. This plan had been brought into battle by an officer of the division, now presumably dead, and had been captured on the battlefield. It was discovered by an officer who could read German, and he had taken it to Freyberg straightaway. It really outlined the entire German plan: the attack on Canea and Suda, and the attack on Maleme. It noted that reinforcements would come by sea to the Maleme area. Further, Galatas, Canea, and Suda were to be captured before dark on the first day. Of course, this had not happened, and Freyberg so noted, with a touch of confidence, in his message to Cairo that night.

But specifically, the finding of the document had some negative results. One was to confirm Freyberg's reluctance to use the Australians near Georgeoupolis to strengthen Campbell at Réthimnon. The document had mentioned sea reinforcement.

What the the document did say very clearly was that it was necessary to capture an airfield in the first few hours. But this point still completely escaped General Freyberg.

What the Germans had done this day was to send in 9,000 parachute and glider troops, thus virtually shooting their wad. General Student had only about two companies of parachute troops left that he could throw into the battle. With all that could be mustered, including headquarters clerks, it came to about 400 more men.

The time for direct action was that night, while the Germans were still relatively off balance and had not put their forces together into a revised plan of attack. In Athens, General Student stayed in his headquarters that day of May 20, waiting for news. Returning pilots from the Maleme area were confident that their drop had been excellent. They had not seen any antiaircraft gunfire. Then the first news came from the ground.

He learned that the Third Parachute Regiment was not moving on Suda; it was stalled. He learned that General Suessmann had been killed before he ever reached Crete. He learned that the Storm Regiment gliders had failed in their mission.

Afternoon came, but with it no better news. General Student did not have any reports of victories, no matter how minor. By evening he knew that the Iráklion detachment had arrived, to be greeted by heavy resistance, and had scattered. At Réthimnon things were no better. Storm was supposed to have won his little battle and be joining the troops at Suda by now, but he obviously was not. He learned of the deaths of half a dozen of his most trusted officers. All the news was bad news. General Student sat in his office in the Hotel Grand Bretagne all night long, waiting.

The only positive hope he could draw from what he learned was that the troops had reached their objectives in every case, although they had not captured them. But the elusive airfield had not been captured. He was disappointed and discouraged, for he knew that many of his fellow generals had believed all along that this was a fool's errand. If Hitler should get that feeling too, then Student's career was behind him.

His feelings were not helped when some of his staff members began to ask late in the evening if he did not want to put together a plan for withdrawal. Withdrawal? How could his paratroops withdraw? He did not have an airfield from which they could be flown out. Were they to swim? Winston Churchill had the situation pegged that night. The Germans were on Crete and they had control of the air. The British were on Crete and they had control of the sea. Neither side had any method of escape. It was a duel to the death.

But negative as most of it was, there was information for the general, except from Réthimnon, where the wireless had failed. He sent a Storch reconnaissance plane to get information, but the plane was captured. Nothing helped.

From Iráklion, from Suda, from the troops south of the river in their strong point, and from Maleme he had reports. As the night wore on, and the disappointment dulled he reconsidered his plan, worrying over a way that he could pull victory out of what seemed to be defeat. And in this he made a tentative decision that the weak point was Maleme. He would concentrate his force the next day on the capture of the airfield at Maleme, and stake everything on its success. Student simply had to have an airfield, and he had to have it immediately. Otherwise the whole German venture would be lost.

So here were the different points of view of the two commanders, about the same situation. The German aggressor had staked the success of his invasion on a wrong set of premises, and had very nearly come to having his whole air landing force destroyed. Now he was desperate to capture an airfield at any price. The Allied defender still did not understand what the Germans had to try to do—and not understanding, he placed no particular value on holding the airfields. Nor did he even consider destroying the runways so that, if the Germans captured a field, it would do them no good.

In London that day, a bit of cautious optimism was in the air. Prime Minister Churchill announced to the House of Commons that the battle had begun in Crete, and later in the morning that the military on Crete had said the situation was in hand. He reported on the loss of the hospital and its recapture later in the morning. The feeling in London was that a serious effort had been made to capture the airfield at Maleme and had failed. The optimism increased as the day went on.

CHAPTER 12

The Long Night

As the darkness deepened over Crete and night settled down, the battlefields became quiet, except for Iráklion, where the Germans were still fighting inside the town. The paratroopers were exhausted after a long, hot day, most of it in brilliant sun with no cover. But then little firefights erupted as stragglers among the Germans tried to find their way to the camp of their friends, and some of the British who had been cut off did the same. Wounded men lay suffering where they had fallen.

Down by the river, the frogs croaked and donkeys brayed. For a time Hill 107 was silent. Lieutenant Colonel Andrew was waiting for the arrival of the reinforcements Brigadier Hargest had promised him hours earlier. Since before dusk he had not heard from his Company C and Headquarters Company, and Company D had vanished, as far as he was concerned. They had not been heard from since morning. He was sure they had been lost, and that the enemy was holding the village of Maleme, and had forces strong enough between the villages of Vlakheronitissa and Xamoudhokhori to push between his eastern and western ridges.

At this point, Andrew was certain that two companies would not be enough to extricate his battalion from its difficulties. If he remained on Hill 107 his positions would be subjected to constant air attacks. He could expect attacks on the ground from three sides. He began to consider a move back to save his two companies.

Sometime after 9 P.M. the first of the reinforcing companies arrived. By that time, Andrew had told Brigadier Hargest of his intention to withdraw to the second ridge held by Company B. Company A had begun to move off Hill 107. He sent the new company to occupy the old Company A positions close to the summit of the hill.

When the company moved to Company B ridge, they were worse off than before. There was no natural cover here, and they had no entrenching tools to create it. If they stayed here they would be attacked mercilessly in the morning by the German bombers and fighters. He decided that he must either go forward or go back to where he had been. If he went back he would have his two companies, the new company from the Twenty-third Battalion that was fresh and augmented by an extra platoon, and the Maori Company. But he decided against it, and in favor of withdrawing his whole force within the perimeters of the Twenty-first and Twenty-third Battalions. So he gave the orders and after 10 P.M. the British troops on Hill 107 moved again. By two in the morning the reinforcing company had also come off Hill 107.

What Andrew did not know was that nearly 200 of his men were still in their trenches on the other side of Hill 107, and the other reinforcing company had already arrived to support them. So there were about 700 British soldiers on the other side, holding their old positions. Other British troops in squad and platoon force were scattered among the Germans along the ridge line, and down toward the eastern bank of the Tavronitis River.

As for the Germans that night, the force was much, much smaller than Andrew believed. Only two groups remained there, separated by about a mile. Altogether they numbered about 600. They were exhausted, thirsty, and mostly without water, and dispirited by the loss of so many of their number.

On the airfield perimeter, one British platoon was still in its trenches and other troops were in position south of the road. Around Pirgos, Andrew's Headquarters Company had been busy that day killing Germans. About 120 parachute troops had landed in and around the village, and most of them had been killed, intercepted by eight Australian artillerymen. A canister from one of the aircraft had yielded a small German field gun.

That night, several of the British companies wandered around in the Hill 107 area, and thus learned that Lieutenant Colonel Andrew and his men had abandoned the hill. The longest march was made by the Maoris, under Captain Rangi Royal. They had left Platanias about 7 P.M. and marched down the coast road, where they encountered small groups of Germans and killed about twenty of them. They lost two men in these encounters. They had gotten lost looking for Company B and wandered around looking for the main road. At 1:30 A.M. they passed through Pirgos, and shouted, but got no response, although Headquarters Company of the battalion was still there. They passed the cemetery and its church and came to the edge of the airfield. They were no more than 200 yards from the Twenty-second Battalion's Company at this point, but neither group found the other. Captain Royal assumed that the Germans had captured the airfield, and continued to search for Lieutenant Colonel Andrew. A scout found the old command post on Hill 107, but said the trenches were empty, so Captain Royal turned back through Pirgos and then met Andrew. The commander directed him to go back to Platanias. The Maoris had marched twelve miles to come to the aid of Lieutenant Colonel Andrew, only to be ordered to march back again and leave the hilltop position deserted. The Germans did not know it, and were too exhausted to find out and try to take the hill. Andrew then began the long march to the positions of the Twenty-third Battalion. Since they would not come to his aid, he abandoned the strongest position on Crete and went to them.

When he arrived, he conferred with Lieutenant Colonel Leckie, Lieutenant Colonel Allen of the Twenty-first Battalion, and other officers. Should they mount a counterattack and retake the hill? They could not pose the question to Brigadier Hargest, for they were out of communication with brigade headquarters. They had to make the decision themselves, knowing that on the following day, if they did not counterattack and retake Hill 107, the Germans would take it—and then the enemy would be able to land aircraft on the airfield. But Lieutenant Colonel Andrew was the senior officer, and the other officers deferred to him. He had no stomach for the counterattack, and the decision was made to hold their present positions, which was as good as giving up the airfield to the Germans.

Just after it became light, Andrew reached brigade headquarters and explained the withdrawal to Brigadier Hargest. They agreed that it was now too late to make a counterattack because if they did they would certainly be attacked in turn by the Luftwaffe. And so the decision was made again to let the

Germans have Hill 107, and to consider a counterattack at the end of the day under the cover of darkness.

Down below the hill, Company C was reduced to about fifty men, because one platoon had been lost and Captain S. H. Johnson was trying to hold out, as he had been ordered to do by Lieutenant Colonel Andrew. But at 4:30 A.M. he discovered that the Germans had moved up the slopes behind him. If he stayed where he was any longer, he would be overrun during the early morning. He moved his men along through snoring Germans and up the hill, until they reached the new perimeter established by Companies A and B.

Finally, early that morning the Germans realized what had happened, and began moving up the hill. They crossed the first line of empty trenches and then another. They came from two sides, and soon they had occupied the vital hill position without a shot being fired.

Dawn broke, and then the sunlight came, and with it, a single JU 52 that swung over the hill without drawing any fire and crossed the runway, skimming the empty trenches that had until recently been held by the British. At last it touched the ground and landed safely near the mouth of the river. It was the first German plane to land on Crete. It carried one of General Student's staff officers, who had been sent to find out, at all costs, what had happened to the troops at Maleme. He had expected to find them in disarray and in desperate straits. Instead he found that, despite their greatly diminished numbers, they controlled the heights above the airport, and the situation was far more favorable than they had any reason to hope a few hours ago. As the staff officer conferred with the paratroop commander, the Twenty-second British Battalion was two miles away, under the protection of the Twenty-third.

Soon the staff officer was on the radio and in contact with Athens, where General Student had the electrifying news that his men actually controlled Hill 107 and now commanded the airfield at Maleme. Student had been wondering where to mount his attack the next day in order to capture the vital airfield. Now he knew. The operation plan was drawn, and sent in short order to the Germans. At about four o'clock, Captain Walter Gericke, commander of the Fourth German Parachute Battalion (or what was left of it) read the order by flashlight. He was to attack the following day, and he would be supported by parachutists who would jump behind the enemy at Maleme.

So the day's battle was now established by the Germans and all they were waiting for was the reinforcement that was promised—plus, if they were lucky, the arrival of the seaborne troops that were on their way. The British, two miles from Hill 107, did not know it, but the events of that fateful night had changed the entire tactical situation in western Crete and Student, who had been nearly desperate at the close of that first deadly day, had now regained all his confidence of victory.

CHAPTER 13

The Germans at Maleme

General Student's staff officer who flew to Maleme very early on the morning of May 21, returned to Athens with the information that the western side of the airstrip was a no-man's-land, and that aircraft could land there. General Student immediately dispatched six more JU 52 aircraft, which landed about two miles west of the airstrip and brought ammunition for the German paratroopers. So by first light of dawn, the British abandonment of Hill 107 had already changed the nature of the battle.

The soldiers of the German Storm Regiment were waiting for those six JU 52s when they landed in the sand near the mouth of the river with the welcome and badly needed ammunition. They arrived at about 8 A.M., and not long afterward, the first of the parachute reinforcements sent by General Student also arrived. They numbered about 350 men. They crossed the Tavronitis on the bridge, where they were attacked by a lone British sniper who hit several of them before he was captured. The Germans then began to move toward the airfield, but were held up by fire from several positions. These had to be Greeks and British troops who had gotten separated from their units and were carrying on a lonely battle, for the British battalions were not engaged with the enemy all day long, but lay in their positions far from the action while the Germans consolidated their grip on the airfield position abandoned by the Twenty-second Battalion. Even with their new strength and weapons and ammunition, the Germans were slow to move. It was evening before they reached the eastern edge of the airfield and captured Maleme village.

That second day, the Luftwaffe came in force to batter the

villages, knowing that they were not held by the parachutists, so that afternoon the air was obscured by dust and debris from furious bombing attacks. The Germans approached the village of Pirgos, and here, in the afternoon, they encountered the first organized resistance of the day from two companies of the Twenty-third Battalion in their trenches. The allied defenders stopped the German advance, and claimed to have shot down 200 Germans.

The figure was exaggerated, but the Germans did run into serious trouble that afternoon. The last two companies of reinforcements parachuted down on the road between Pirgos and Platanias. Some of the men fell into the sea, where their heavy equipment dragged them down to drown. Those who came down on the land arrived in the vicinity of the Engineer Battalion and the Maoris, and not many of these troops survived the storm of fire loaded on them. In one company, all of the officers and noncommissioned officers were lost. From the second company, one officer and eighty men managed to reach Pirgos and take shelter in the houses there and in the bamboo that lined the road.

Late in the afternoon, the full force of the British error in abandoning Hill 107 was beginning to be felt. When General Student learned the details of the landing his staff officer had made on the corner of the airfield at Maleme, he decided to send a battalion of his Mountain troops, 800 strong, to be carried in by JU 52s and landed on the airfield. Some crash landed on the beach and some landed south of the airfield, but most landed on the field, jumped out, and made for cover. Their casualties were very light, because the nearest New Zealanders were a mile and a half from the runway, and the range was too great for their machine guns and mortars. For a time, the British artillery fired on the planes and the men getting out of them. But on Hill 107, the Germans watched the muzzle blasts of the British guns and radioed the Luftwaffe their positions, so the Messerschmitts kept flashing down to attack the guns. It was a lesson in the value of good communications over bad. Half the artillerymen were killed or wounded, but the survivors continued to fire the Italian 75 mm guns. They set fire to some of the German planes and wrecked others, about twenty in all. But the majority of the German planes got going again and returned to their air bases in Greece that afternoon.

By seven o'clock that second night, the Germans were moving along the road to prevent the British from counterattacking and regaining control of the airfield. In Athens, General Student was much encouraged by the day's events and confident that he would win a victory in Crete. But in Germany, Goering and Hitler were upset by the revelation of the heavy casualties suffered by the parachutists on the first day. And in Crete, the Germans waited uneasily for the strong British counterattack that they expected and were not sure they could survive. But Student was confident that his men could hold out until the reinforcements came in. Thousands of parachutists and Mountain troops were on their way by sea, with heavy weapons. But the problem at the moment was the same as it had been, because of the losses of both new men and old during the day's fighting. The Germans had scarcely 2,000 men on Crete at the moment, and they still had no heavy weapons. With this force they had to retain control of the Maleme airfield so that reinforcements could come in the next day.

The German commander decided that the major threat to his success lay in the nine field guns that had been shelling the airfield that day, and he opted to try to destroy them. The British, meanwhile, had been dithering all day, and continued to be apprehensive and cautious in their every move. Some 14,000 men were available at Suda alone, and they were not even considered by the commanders. General Freyberg held a meeting to discuss what he believed to be the two main problems. One was the recapture of Maleme, and the other and more vital the defense of the coast against the German landing they expected this night. He and his subordinate commanders agreed to use two battalions to recapture Maleme. It was not nearly a large enough force, but General Freyberg did not order more men. His uppermost concern, as it had been from the beginning, was the sea invasion he expected at any moment. He knew that the Germans had used the Maleme airfield that day, but he did not consider that to be significant, because he thought they were capable of landing their planes almost anywhere on the island.

Admiral Sir Andrew Cunningham, the commander of the naval forces in Egypt, was well aware of the threat from the sea. His long-range reconnaissance aircraft had reported for several days that groups of small craft were moving southwest through the Greek islands. Since the day before, he had a small patrolling force off the north coast of the island. They had been attacked by German and Italian bombers, and the destroyer *Juno* had been sunk and the cruiser *Ajax* damaged. During the daylight hours the vessels had moved away from Crete but they were back again on the night of May 21, looking for the flotilla of reinforcement.

Two invasion flotillas, made up mostly of Greek caiques carrying a hundred men each, were at sea. During the daylight hours, they were protected by the Luftwaffe, but at night they had no protection because the Italian navy, having suffered serious losses in encounters with the British fleet, refused to bring a protective force to Crete.

On the night before, the German invasion force coming to the west had reached the island of Milos, seventy miles from Crete. On the morning of May 21, it had set out again at dawn with the small escort that the Italians had supplied. All went well in the morning, but then the wind died and the sailing caiques drifted aimlessly. That night, the British squadron of destroyers and cruisers found the flotilla bound for Maleme about 20 miles north of Canea, and sank about a dozen vessels, including several small steamers crammed to the gunwales with German infantry. Many of the Germans drowned, but some managed to stay afloat, and some of the caiques escaped in the darkness and made it to land. But very few of these troops reached Crete.

That same night, the British eastern squadron of cruisers and destroyers came upon the first ships of the second German flotilla. But they did not come within range of the main German force until ten o'clock in the morning, and by that time, the Luftwaffe was in the air. Rear Admiral E. King, the officer in charge of the force, decided that the danger from the Luftwaffe was too great to risk, and withdrew. But the Luftwaffe was active that day and attacked the British forces, sinking the destroyer *Greyhound*, the cruisers *Fiji*, and *Gloucester*, and damaging the cruiser *Warspite*.

On Crete at 7 P.M., Brigadier Hargest learned that he was to begin the attack on the airfield that night. He would have his own troops and the Twentieth Battalion of New Zealanders, with three tanks and the artillery in support. At midnight, the Royal Air Force promised to put in its first appearance over Crete since the battle began and drop some bombs.

Brigadier Hargest decided to use the Twentieth Battalion

and the Maoris west of Platanias, to advance on Pirgos, and then to the slopes of Hill 107. The Twenty-first Battalion would occupy the high ground farther south. Although the village of Pirgos was full of Germans hiding in the houses, the Twenty-third Battalion, whose area this was, was not ordered to clear the Germans out. And the counterattack was to be made by what amounted to a single battalion.

Then another negative factor arose. General Freyberg ordered the Twentieth to stay in position, guarding the coast against the sea invasion he expected, until it could be relieved by the Australian battalion from Georgeoupolis. The trucks that brought the Australians to the area would then move the Twentieth Battalion to its kickoff point for the attack. But the Australians were delayed in their relief of the battalion. They were bombed and strafed by the Luftwaffe on the road. The last of the battalion did not reach Canea until after darkness had begun to fall. Then the units got lost and were misdirected, so that they did not come into position with the Twentieth Battalion until midnight.

By midnight, the Germans were all but defeated on Crete, all that was needed was a strong driving counterattack to knock them off Hill 107 and regain control of the airfield. Their seaborne effort had failed. The only troops on the island were paratroopers and mountain troops with few weapons, no tanks, and no artillery to speak of. Only a few hundred troops stood between the airfield and the thousands of British troops who could attack. A victory for the Germans still seemed completely unlikely.

It had become quite apparent relatively early in the night that the Royal Navy was engaging the German reinforcement flotilla, and that the German reinforcement from the sea was not going to arrive. But Brigadier Puttick, when asked to release the Twentieth Battalion because there would be no attack from the sea, refused to do so, and the hours continued to pass. All concerned in the assault except the brigadiers involved seemed to understand that the attack on Hill 107 had to be accomplished at night, or the Luftwaffe would intervene and make it either impossible or extremely costly. It was two o'clock in the morning before the commander of the Twentieth Battalion reached brigade headquarters and could confer with

Brigadier Hargest, who seemed to be so exhausted he did not know what he was doing.

By 3 A.M., only two of the companies of the Twentieth had been moved up to the point of departure. Even if the men started immediately, they would not reach the airfield until daylight, and Hargest then decided to see if the attack could be called off. He telephoned Brigadier Puttick at division headquarters and was told that the attack must proceed no matter what. So the first two companies of the Twentieth Battalion set off alone, with the promise that the others would follow. The Maoris had been fidgeting for four hours, before they finally started to move at 3:30 A.M.

The troops moved slowly, hampered by encounters with small pockets of Germans near the shore. Along the road, they ran into mines and booby traps set by the Germans. But they continued on, reaching the bamboo growth north of Pirgos at about dawn. The Maoris moved south of the road, joined by armed Cretans, who had been waiting for this counterattack. The three tanks rumbled along the road. But it was clear daylight before the Maoris reached the village of Dhaskaliana, and they could see more German aircraft landing on the airfield still two miles away. As they moved through Pirgos, they flushed more Germans out of the houses.

The men of the Twentieth encountered a large group of survivors from the parachute drops of the previous day. The sun was shining brightly on the airfield as they reached the edge of it. It was bright morning, and the Me-109s were diving on them as they moved. Most of their officers had been killed, and they were drawing fire from the German machine guns on Hill 107. There was no protection here, and the men had to withdraw into the bamboo for cover.

The tanks, supported by a few infantrymen, moved up the road to the crossroads east of Pirgos. When the leading tank reached the central street, it was fired upon and destroyed by two field guns located in the cemetery. The second tank, attacked by Me-109s, crashed into the bamboo and stopped.

One company commander of the Twentieth Battalion seemed to have misunderstood his orders and withdrew to Platanias with his company and part of another, leaving a large hole in the British line.

All this while, the German planes were landing on the airfield and disgorging new troops to enter the battle. Still, the German effort was within a short distance of failure. That morning, the counterattack had petered out, but the Germans still had only about 2,000 troops capable of fighting. They had failed at Iráklion and Réthimnon to take their objectives. Freyberg had at least 13,000 fighting troops available, and the Greeks and Cretans had certainly proved themselves, despite all the misgivings of the British high command. All the British had to do was fight. The men knew it, but their high officers did not seem to realize this.

The Germans, from General Student down, seemed much more aware of what was happening on Crete than the British high command. On the morning of the twenty-second, Student knew that he had been right to stake everything on the Maleme capture, and he now decided to send in the whole Fifth Mountain Division. The eastern flotilla of the seaborne invasion was recalled to Piraeus so the troops could be shipped in by air. So much for General Freyberg's fear of the seaborne invasion. So all the German effort now would be directed at Maleme, and the other Germans on the island would fight holding actions.

Colonel Heidrich had about 1,200 men attacking the heights near Galatas. They were the survivors of the Third Parachute Regiment, augmented by men who had arrived the day before. He was driving them to attack, while still holding the prison and the prison area. That morning of May 22, he sent a detachment of 150 men to attack at Galatas again. The German concern about the artillery shelling the airfield became less as the day wore on and the Luftwaffe found and silenced several of the guns.

That evening, after General Student had decided to place all his bets on the battle at Maleme, he sent in Lieutenant General J. Ringel to take command of the troops there. One of his orders was to the Mountain troops to destroy the British artillery. Student expected to make much greater use of the Maleme airfield the next day, after this was accomplished. But before General Ringel could arrive, there was a whole day's fighting to be done.

As the Maoris approached Hill 107, they came under heavy fire from the machine guns there. They also were hit by fire from houses and hiding places along the roadside, where more survivors of the previous day's drop had holed up. The Maoris struggled forward until the combination of fire from the ground and the strafing by the Me-109s became too great.

By this time it was afternoon. An officer went back to seek support from the Twenty-second and Twenty-third battalions, but got nothing. Lieutenant Colonel Leckie and Lieutenant Colonel Andrew were not willing to risk their men in this fight. The officers were paralyzed with fear of the Luftwaffe. They believed the whole Twentieth Battalion had withdrawn with that one officer, and they said they must have more infantry, artillery, and air support to renew the counterattack. Since it was patently impossible to get either air support or more artillery, the attack was now doomed to be a failure.

The soldiers had much more spirit than their leaders. One platoon of the Twenty-third Battalion joined the Maoris without orders. The soldiers made their way along across country, through Maleme village and to the slopes of Hill 107. They found themselves among Germans, but not very many Germans. With any support they thought they could recapture the hill, But their leaders were too dispirited to offer such support. So the platoon had to stop its attack and make its way back to the other British troops.

By late afternoon of May 22, the Maoris had also been forced to withdraw to the valley south of Pirgos. There they encountered a German patrol of about platoon strength, which they eliminated with a bayonet charge that took them to a ridge. Later the Germans began an attack, and the Maoris waited, then rose and began to move forward with fixed bayonets, firing from the hip. They reached the Germans and began a bayonet attack. The Germans turned and fled. The Maoris walked back through the fallen Germans to their defense line. That morning, Lieutenant Colonel Allen of the Twenty-first had decided to make an attempt with his battalion to advance and take Hill 107. As his troops reached the enemy line, the Luftwaffe stopped their attacks. They pressed forward through two villages, and came very near the summit of Hill 107.

Some of the men of the Twenty-second Battalion joined the fight, and reached their old positions on the east bank of the Tavronitis River. But now they faced fresh German troops who had come in during the day and the night before. Lieutenant Colonel Allen was forced to withdraw to a ridge, called Vineyard Ridge. But he had proved something that the British commanders still did not seem to realize, that it was possible to attack in spite of the Luftwaffe, and that when they engaged the Germans the Luftwaffe stopped its attacks lest it hit German troops. It was apparent at this point that the commanders' fear of the Luftwaffe was unreasonable and much too intense. It was becoming a major factor in the battle for Crete.

In the area between Pirgos and Platanias, many Germans surrendered that day. With no water and no food, they were becoming desperate, and their knowledge that the sea reenforcement had failed the night before destroyed their spirit. Early in the day, the Engineer Detachment took sixty-five prisoners. The British artillery continued to shell the airfield at Maleme, although the gunners had no contact with the British infantry and thus could not give them any support.

The Germans, who had been expecting a strong counterattack ever since they first landed on Crete, were surprised that it had not come. They did not regard what had happened this day as a serious counterattack. Their confidence was increasing with every planeload of new troops that landed on the airfield.

At brigade headquarters, Brigadier Hargest spent most of the day living in a fool's paradise, even though he learned very early that the tanks had failed in their attack, and the promised support of the Royal Air Force had never appeared. Neither had artillery that was supposed to move up to Platanias. Hargest had very little information, and no communication with the battalions. All he really knew was what he could see through his field glasses, and that was not much. The airfield was five miles away and hidden by the hills.

But once in a while, a soldier or an officer appeared from the fighting area, and the reports that Hargest got were that affairs were moving smoothly enough. At one point, he believed that the attack had succeeded and the British had occupied the airfield, and he so announced by radio to Brigadier Puttick at division headquarters. But by one o'clock in the afternoon he began to receive some more truthful, and more discouraging, reports. First, he had to report to Division that the troops had not gotten as far forward on the left as he had believed. Later he learned that the whole brigade was back on a defense line south of Pirgos and that no real progress had been made all day long.

At divisional headquarters and at General Freyberg's headquarters nobody seemed to care very much about the failure of the counterattack at Maleme. The officers were all preoccupied with the defense of the coast against a seaborne landing, and were not counting the aircraft that came in to Maleme airfield all day long, bringing more German troops. Brigadier Puttick was suffering badly from the Luftwaffe syndrome that seemed to affect the whole high command since the days of the Battle of Britain. They persistently overestimated Luftwaffe strength, aggressiveness, and organization.

At Galatas the New Zealanders were attacked by the Germans again in the evening of May 22. Now the remnants of the Sixth Greek Regiment under Captain Michael Forrester came into the battle as the Germans were attacking the Divisional Petrol Company there. Leading his Greeks, he came rushing forward, yelling. The Germans turned and ran, and the British and the Greeks settled down. Below at Pink Hill, a group of fifty Greeks attacked some houses and killed all the Germans in them. In fact, all over the island the Cretans were fighting the Germans. In Iráklion, the Greeks and Cretans finally drove the Germans from the quays and off to the west out of the city.

Before nightfall on that second day, the bodies of 950 dead Germans had been collected in the British sector and another 300 were piled up in the Greek sector. Many more were scattered about the island. Of the 2,000 men who had jumped on the first day, three quarters were dead.

By that evening, after some rough hours, the British at Réthimnon were firmly in control. The Germans had captured Hill A and seemed likely to take the Réthimnon airfield, but Lieutenant Colonel Campbell had thrown in his reserve without compunction and had retaken the hill, in sharp contrast to the actions of the battalions fighting around Maleme.

All day long the Junkets transports had flown into Maleme and unloaded three battalions of German Mountain Troops. The airfield was littered with wrecked aircraft, but cleared by the Germans with the use of prisoners who were ordered to unload the planes of ammunition and supplies as well. When some prisoners refused to do so, they were shot in front of the other prisoners as an example. The Germans were also furious with the Cretans for fighting them. In all their conquests so far in this war, they had never seen this sort of fury from civilian populations, and they were indignant.

So the darkness came down on the night of May 22, and

the British still had the power to win a victory if they would only mount their counterattack this night. The German strength on Hill 107 was still not very great, although the British had not made an effort to discover how great it was. What General Student and his field commanders were hoping was that they could hold out long enough for him to bring in enough reinforcements to tip the scale of the battle.

CHAPTER 14

The Tide Changes

On May 22, General Freyberg began to have some understanding of the German tactics in Crete as he watched the JU 52s coming in and going out of the Maleme airfield. He was fed optimistic news about the counterattack that was too little and too late to be effective until afternoon, when Brigadier Hargest stopped making his optimistic statements. He began to realize what the enemy control of that airfield meant. Early in the afternoon, he asked the New Zealand Division to estimate the number of troops landed at Maleme. He did not get the answer until nearly seven o'clock that night. Then it was wildly inaccurate. He could not even get accurate figures on how many aircraft had landed at the field that day, because nobody had been counting until after lunch, when it suddenly began to strike the senior officers that the landings were important.

Much later General Freyberg was to get estimates that 2,400 parachutists had landed on May 20. On May 21, 300 more paratroopers and 300 airborne troops joined them, and on May 22, another 1,500 airborne troops arrived, plus many supplies. So that evening, General Freyberg gave orders that there was to be another counterattack to dislodge the Germans from Hill 107 and the airfield at Maleme. The attack would be made by the Fourth Brigade.

But when Brigadier Puttick received these orders he was already getting information about increased German activity in the area between the Fourth and Fifth Brigades. There were indications that the force in the Prison area was probing northward and might attack. Puttick thought it was already too late to counterattack, and he called General Freyberg and suggested that the Fifth Brigade be withdrawn. If this were to happen, then the Germans would have untrammeled use of the airfield the next day because the Fifth Brigade would have moved back five miles.

Freyberg appeared to agree, and he sent Brigadier Stewart to confer with Puttick. By ten o'clock that night it was all decided. The Fifth Brigade would move to the line of the road east of Platanias and link up with the Tenth Brigade. The disorganized Twenty-second Battalion would join the Fourth Brigade, and the Australians would join the New Zealanders. More than forty vehicles would be used in what they now called a "salvage" operation. Gone were all thoughts of attacking the numerically inferior Germans and beating them. The whole ambience now, as always, was turned to defense, not offense. What was important, these brigadiers decided, was to present a solid front to the Germans. That seemed to be more important than winning.

This, in a sense, was the last chance. The British fighting men in the line were ready and full of fight. They were also determined and skillful fighters. If the Germans were not attacked this night, and decisively beaten as they must be simply by force of numbers in a serious attack, then as Brigadier Stewart said later, the defeat of the British in Crete was virtually accepted.

So General Freyberg had ordered an attack, Brigadier Puttick had decided against it and undermined the entire British position, and Freyberg had let him do it.

The fact was that the defensive mentality that had settled on the senior British officers caused them to magnify every German success and forget every German loss.

When the units were told that they were going to withdraw, there was shock and consternation among the men. They thought the fight had been going well. They had killed many, many Germans. But at one o'clock in the morning on May 23, they were told to move out and retreat. As they retreated, there were no signs of the Germans, and no firing at them. So without understanding why, they retreated back five miles and left Maleme and the airfield to the Germans. By morning they were eight miles from Maleme airfield.

At first light the Germans were not slow to take advantage of this new opportunity thrust into their hands by a mismanaged, confused enemy that was several times as strong as their own force. The Storm Regiment began to move cautiously forward from Pirgos, and passed through the area where the Third Battalion had been destroyed. These surviving troops were reduced to the strength of a single battalion, and they were exhausted. For three days they had been fighting, and they knew there were no reserves. So they kept going.

By 7 A.M., the Germans were moving forward without any opposition along the coast road. Soon they caught up with the Maoris, who were covering the retreat, and fighting began.

Before the Germans was Platanias, whose steep cliffs barred the way to the naval base at Suda. Now that the British had abandoned their fortified positions under cover, and were out in the open, they became easy prey for the Luftwaffe, which was this morning beginning its assault again.

The Germans on the ground made no effort to attack the British this day. But the Luftwaffe was out and the fighters patrolled the coast road.

General Freyberg was now becoming concerned about resupply of his forces. With the Germans in control of the airfield and able to bring in more men, he realized that the time when the fight might have been won quickly was over. And the Germans controlled the skies, so that the Royal Navy said it would be impossible to resupply Crete through Suda Bay. The new port that everyone was talking about was Tymbaki, a little port on the south coast, on the Gulf of Mesara. General Freyberg was beginning to have the sinking feeling that the battle was already lost. Now messages from his friend, the prime minister in London, showed how little the officials in London understood the situation. Churchill cabled General Wavell saying the battle for Crete must be won, even if it meant fighting on the island indefinitely, for this would keep the Germans occupied and help the British in the western desert. He said he hoped Wavell would reinforce Crete every night and send more tanks. Churchill also inquired if it would not be possible to recapture the lost airfield. How little they understood in London that the opportunities for victory had been thrown away by disorganization and excessive caution! They still did not understand what had happened in Crete. Not only the politicians, but the chiefs of staff of the services as well misunderstood the situation. They, too, insisted that Wavell reinforce the island and said that if he did so, the Germans might get tired of the effort and quit. They called for reinforcements to be sent to the island to wipe out the Germans before they could be seriously reinforced. "The vital importance of this battle is well known to you," they said to Wavell, "and great risks must be accepted to ensure our success."

But here the brigade commanders had let the side down. They had not been willing to take the "great risks". Had they attacked on either of the first two nights there would have been minimal risk, because the British forces so overwhelmingly outnumbered the enemy. London did not know that the British in Crete had thrown away one advantage after another.

Admiral Cunningham regarded Crete as an already lost cause, but he continued to do his best with supplies. On the night of May 23, two destroyers slipped into Suda Bay with ammunition and other supplies, unloaded and slipped out again well before dawn.

On May 24, for the first time the British had a little help from the RAF. Several Blenheim bombers bombed the Maleme airfield. The attack was good for British morale on the island, but it really did virtually no damage to the Germans. But the RAF reluctance to participate in this battle was reinforced when twelve Hurricane fighters were dispatched to Iráklion. Two of them were shot down by British naval gunners who could not believe their eyes when they saw RAF planes in the air and thought they were German. Three more were so badly damaged by friendly fire that they limped back to Africa. One of this first flight reached Iráklion, where it was destroyed on the ground by the Luftwaffe. The second flight of six came in, and five were shot down by the Germans before they could land. The sixth survived for a time, but obviously made no difference in the outcome of the struggle.

In Cairo and in London this news was scarcely known. Hopes continued strong. Wavell hoped that the line at Galatas could hold, and that a striking force could be assembled from Iráklion and Réthimnon. Cairo would try then to bring reinforcements in to Tymbaki.

But at Réthimnon the British were engaged by a German force, and had been for three days, and Lieutenant Colonel Campbell had another worry. He had many wounded on his hands, most of them German, and only enough food supply for four more days. He did not lose heart, and continued to keep abreast of developments by riding around the area on his motorcycle. The Me-109s did not trouble with a single cyclist, so he was safe enough. In fact, the Luftwaffe was still having great difficulty in this battle in distinguishing friend from foe, and was bombing and strafing the Germans more than the British. Here the Germans had no radio, and could not communicate with the airmen.

In this area the Germans had entrenched themselves in an olive oil factory at Stavromenos. The Greeks and Australians attacked them on May 23, but the attack failed and the troops had to withdraw under cover of darkness. On the other flank, the British were harried all that day by the Luftwaffe, with the Me-109s causing nearly forty casualties with their machine gun fire. After the exhausting day, the parachutists attacked with the setting sun behind them and suffered very heavy casualties. Two days later, Campbell ordered another attack on the olive oil factory, and this one succeeded. The Allies captured nearly a hundred prisoners. But the Germans continued to hang on in this area, and nothing Campbell could do with his limited weapons would force them out of the houses where they had taken possession along the road. Thus, the Germans maintained their roadblock at Réthimnon, although that was all they could do. The plight of the Germans here was indicative of what would have happened to the whole German force had the brigade commanders been as assertive as was Lieutenant Colonel Campbell. He was whittling away at the German force every day without a letup.

The Germans who had attacked at Iráklion were also suffering. On the second evening of the battle, 150 parachutists had been dropped here, and on the morning of May 24, 400 Germans were dropped west and south of Iráklion. But these were the only reinforcements the Iráklion survivors of the first day were to get. The Luftwaffe was of little help to the Germans here, because its efforts were being expended on the west side of the island, and against the British fleet. Some attempts at resupply by air were made, but the Greeks managed to garner most of the supply drops.

By the end of the third day, the wireless sets were failing and ammunition was running short. Contact between the units could be maintained only by runner, but the Germans were able to do this, unlike the British, who failed signally in this respect. The Germans wondered how long they could hold out, and in Athens, General Student wondered too. Airborne units were not meant for this kind of work. They were shock troops, which depended on quick support from other units, especially from artillery and armor. Here on Crete the Germans had neither, nor did they have much supply. As the British continued to worry about German seaborne invasion, so did the Germans worry that the Royal Navy might bring in reinforcements with tanks and heavy artillery. General Student was worried about the situation of his troops in Iráklion and Réthimnon and wanted to do something about it. But whatever was done had to be organized from Maleme, for that is where the German strength was pouring in.

Brigadier Chappell at Iráklion had given away completely to inertia. As the days went on, he mounted no attacks whatsoever, although his strength had increased since the first day. Two tanks had come up from Tymbaki, where they had been landed with the Argyll and Sutherland Highlanders, sent as reinforcements from Egypt. The Iráklion garrison then came to over 3,000 British and Australian troops, 1,000 other British troops of mixed units, three Greek battalions, and hundreds of armed Cretans. There was now plenty of equipment and rifles, captured from the dead Germans and the air drops. And to face them here were only a thousand German paratroops, tired, hungry, thirsty, and dispirited. Any serious attack by Brigadier Chappell on the Germans must certainly have succeeded. But no such attack materialized on May 23 or May 24, and on the afternoon of May 25, after General Student ordered help for his men at Iráklion, the Luftwaffe bombers came and reduced the town to rubble.

That night, General Student ordered Major Schulz, who had succeeded in command of the German remnants, to lead his group of parachutists on a long night march eastward to join the rest of the Germans and consolidate their positions. They captured an important hill called Apex Hill after suffering heavy losses. From this position they could command the airfield at Iráklion. They left only a handful of men in the west to care for the wounded, and to maintain the fiction that the German position there was strong. The British command did not have the energy to discover the facts. Instead, Brigadier Chappell lived on rumors. The British saw parachutes falling east of the town, and assumed that they carried parachute troops. They did not; they carried supplies for the Germans, much of which fell into Greek hands. So the word was sent to General Freyberg and to Wavell in Cairo that the Germans were building up their force at Iráklion, when there was no truth at all in the statement. Quite to the contrary, the Iráklion contingent of Germans grew weaker every day. Colonel Brauer, who had made the original landing with his men east of the airfield, had only eighty men left of his original eight hundred, and they had no food and little ammunition by May 24.

Furthermore, Brigadier Chappell had plenty of strength to send a force to Réthimnon to assist Lieutenant Colonel Campbell, who was fighting the only real war being fought in Crete, and had five hundred German prisoners in his stockade. But Brigadier Chappell said the road was blocked by the Germans, and he did not try to find out how many Germans. It was true there was a German roadblock between Iráklion and Réthimnon, but it was manned by a handful of paratroopers who could have been dispersed in an hour's fighting by a single battalion. What happened? Nothing.

On May 22, the Germans had been enraged by the killing of German soldiers by Cretan guerrillas who were members of no army and had no uniforms. On May 23, they announced from Athens that Cretans found bearing arms would be shot on sight. At the moment these were empty promises of revenge, but they did not long remain that way. On May 24 the Germans systematically began to demolish Cretan towns and villages, to punish the civil population for not greeting them with open arms. That day Canea was destroyed, and the dive bombers and fighters came back to strafe the civilian refugees who fled from the ruins.

On the west side of the island, where the action was taking place, on May 24 it was quiet from the Prison valley to the sea. The British had evacuated, leaving the Germans in control, and the Germans were consolidating their gains and securing the important high ground.

The British were now beginning to suffer from lack of supplies. The Luftwaffe prevented the daylight supply of Crete through Suda, and while General Freyberg estimated that he needed 500 tons of supply per day to keep going, he was getting only about 100 tons through the southern ports.

By May 24, the British had a fairly accurate assessment of the German landings. So far, about 15,000 men had been landed on Crete, 6,500 in the Maleme area, 6,000 in the Prison valley and Réthimnon, and the rest at Iráklion. But the German casualties were underestimated to be less than 3,500. As far as the defenders were concerned, their casualties had been extremely light because they had not fought a major engagement. Altogether, the British casualties were fewer than 2,000, three-quarters of them wounded.

But the time had nearly come when the Germans would go on the all-out offensive. It was signalled on the night of May 24, when Radio Berlin and the other German radio stations announced for the first time that land fighting was going on in Crete. Until this time, the Wehrmacht had been so uncertain of the outcome of the German landings that the whole Crete adventure had been kept secret. The announcement of the fighting showed that the German high command was now fairly confident of victory. And the British command on Crete was now looking defeat in the face.

That night General Freyberg moved his headquarters to the south shore of Suda Bay for safety. His communique to Wavell called for reinforcements by infantry, tanks, and strikes by the Royal Air Force and the Royal Navy. He got none of these.

General Ringel, the new commander of the German forces at Maleme, was now waiting for reinforcements to come in by air so that he could launch an attack on Galatas, the capture of which should put him in control of Suda Bay. But in Athens, General Student was having his problems. Demands were coming from Berlin that Air Fleet IV should go to the eastern front, where it was needed for the attack on Russia. Otherwise, said the Wehrmacht high command, the Russian invasion must be delayed. They had expected the fighting in Crete to be all over on May 25, based on General Student's estimates. Now Student had to tell General Ringel that he could not wait. After May 25, he was not sure how much longer he could maintain the air support by the Luftwaffe.

Now that most of the Fifth Mountain Division had arrived at Maleme, Ringel was planning on a battle for May 25. He would attack at Galatas and break the British line. At the same time, he would send a flanking movement through the mountains of southeastern Crete.

The striking force would be two battalions of the Mountain Infantry, fresh troops just brought in by air to the field at Maleme, with plenty of arms. Each company had twenty heavy and light machine guns, rifles, and all the grenades a man could carry. Farther back was his reserve, two more battalions of fresh troops and a regiment of artillery.

The attack would be made from Hill 107 north to Galatas, with the Prison valley on the right. The road wound its way up the mountain to a hill on which a cemetery stood, called Cemetery Hill, and next to it were Ruin Hill, Pink Hill and Wheat Hill. On the far side was the road that ran up to the village of Galatas on its ridge top.

The British had brought up the New Zealand Eighteenth Battalion, about 400 fresh troops, but they were scattered on a front that stretched a mile and a half from the shore to the west side of Galatas. Behind was the Fifth Brigade.

The biggest problem of the British here at Galatas was shortage of ammunition. They had fewer than a hundred mortar shells and very few grenades.

On May 24, the troops had a respite from the daily attacks of the Luftwaffe fighters and bombers as the German air force concentrated its efforts on the destruction of Canea. That night was quiet, except for an unusual amount of German signalling by flares in the west. The New Zealanders on the line slept. Soon it would be morning, and the sixth day of a battle that General Student had expected to be over in five days.

CHAPTER 15

Day of Battle

The morning of May 25 dawned with the Luftwaffe coming in, in strength as usual, all over the island. But at about one o'clock in the afternoon, the Germans began to concentrate their air attack on Galatas itself. After a few minutes of aerial bombardment, the German line began to move forward, the men in green seeking cover as they came behind olive trees, outcroppings of rock, and thickets. The men of the Eighteenth Battalion began firing and dropped many of the enemy, but they continued to advance.

As the afternoon dragged on, the German pressure forced Lieutenant Colonel Gray to retreat from Ruin Hill, the most western of the hills. As soon as the New Zealanders moved off the hill the Germans moved on, and then could give enfilading fire to the British troops farther north.

The commander of the Eighteenth Battalion company in the area south of the coast road was killed, and the Germans pressed in on his company. Lieutenant Colonel Gray rushed to the scene with all the men he could collect—cooks, clerks, and other specialists—but they could not help. All but twelve of that company were either killed or captured by the Germans.

The Germans threatened to go down the road to Canea, but Brigadier Kippenberger sent a hundred men down to block the road, and they did.

As the sun began to set, the German pressure increased against the center of the line. On Wheat Hill, the defenders asked for permission to withdraw, but Kippenberger refused. A little while later, another runner came and again asked permission to withdraw, and again Kippenberger refused. But by seven o'clock, the Germans were on the hill and the survivors were falling back. The German grenades and mortars, all brought in by transport plane to the Maleme airfield, were the most effective weapon this afternoon. In the last fading light of day, the German Mountain troops gained the summit of Cemetery Hill, and could see beyond the ruins of Canea and the water in Suda Bay.

The Germans were now on the foot of Pink Hill, but Galatas was still holding. After the withdrawal of the Eighteenth Battalion from the other hills, the gunfire against this position on Pink Hill became intense. This defense was led by a captain who was normally the supply officer of the division. He held as long as he could, and then moved his troops back to the shelter of Galatas.

North of them, the Eighteenth Battalion was nearly shattered, and the men were falling back as the Germans pressed on them. Their right flank was endangered from the rear, where the Germans had gotten behind them. Kippenberger had called for reinforcements, and Brigadier Hargest had finally pulled himself together enough to send some. So had Brigadier Inglis, commander of the Fourth Brigade, which so far had been almost unsullied by battle, in the general disposition of the senior officers to avoid battle until now. The Fourth Brigade band was about the first to arrive, and Kippenberger lined the men up along a stone wall that ran north from Galatas under the top of the hill. He moved the shattered remnants of the Eighteenth Battalion east along the road and directed it to go into reserve near the white church at Karatsos. As elements of the Fourth and Fifth Brigades continued to come up, Kippenberger put them along the coast road and plugged up the gap in the center of the line. The Germans began to move among the houses, but the Australian artillerymen not far from the point, who had four Italian 75 mm guns, began firing on them, and the Germans quickly retreated.

The men of the Twenty-third Battalion had been waiting all day, and at 5 P.M. they were called upon to move. They marched up the road toward Galatas, and mounted the last rise. There, Lieutenant Colonel Leckie was wounded in the leg by a machine gun bullet. They left him lying there and moved to where Brigadier Kippenberger was waiting for them. By this time, the Luftwaffe planes were leaving Cretan air for their air bases, and the battlefield was much quieter. The German flares punctuated the gathering dusk above them.

Lieutenant Farran had made a reconnaissance of Galatas village in his tank, and he reported that the Germans were there in some strength, occupying many of the houses. Brigadier Kippenberger decided that Galatas must be recaptured, and ordered Farran to lead the way with his two tanks. The men of the Twenty-third now commanded by Major Thomason, would follow, one company on each side of the road. As they assembled, they gained reinforcements, stragglers from other units who wanted to join in this desperate attack.

It was growing dark and the stars shone above them. German tracers crackled across the air above their heads, and they heard occasional shots from solitary rifles from the village ahead of them. They fixed bayonets and waited.

Lieutenant Farran got his tanks ready. Two of his tankers were wounded, and they were replaced by engineer volunteers who could manage machine guns. So it was after 8 P.M. when the attackers were ready to move. Brigadier Kippenberger gave the order, and Farran climbed into his lead tank and raced its engine, then pulled out, followed by the second tank. They moved up the road. Two hundred men followed them.

The tanks burst into the village in a cloud of dust, and the men behind began to shout. The racket was heard on the other side of the village by Lieutenant Colonel Gray, and as far as the side of Prison valley by the Germans, who knew it for what it was, a battle cry.

Fire began to spurt from guns in the houses of the village. German mortars were firing, too, but they did *not* have the range, and the shells crashed harmlessly behind the British troops. One by one, the attackers assailed the houses, trapping many Germans inside. They hurled grenades through the windows. The fighting was hand-to-hand, with pistol, bayonet, and knife and grenade as much as with rifle fire. They passed Lieutenant Farran, who had been wounded and was out of his tank and on the road.

The men of the Twenty-third Battalion surged on. A machine gun held up the attack. One private with a Bren gun moved forward, firing steadily from the hip. Around behind the machine gun, the attackers outflanked the German gunners and killed them and the private.

The Germans formed up at one strong point in a house. The British began hurling grenades, and one burst in the doorway.

The Germans dived out of the house and the British shot them down.

One platoon encountered resistance at the village school but brought it to an end with grenades. By this time, the Germans were running away from the fierce onslaught. The men of the Twenty-third kept driving on until they cleared the village and stood on the top of the prison road.

They had won a victory, but most of their officers and non-commissioned officers were dead or wounded. But they had saved the units trapped by the Germans on this side of the village. Brigadier Kippenberger went back to report to Brigadier Inglis that the fight had been successful.

When he reached Fourth Brigade headquarters, he found Brigadier Inglis conferring with his battalion commanders at the command post. They talked about the next move, and Inglis sent a message to Brigadier Puttick, the division commander, to come and discuss the future. Kippenberger said that at least two fresh battalions would be needed, and they hoped that Puttick and Freyberg would agree to send them. But Puttick did not come. Instead he sent a staff officer, who had nothing to offer. Most of all, he had no reinforcements to offer.

All the British had to work with was the Maori unit, now reduced to a strength of under five hundred men. And something must be done before morning to restore the British right flank, otherwise Galatas, having been won against such odds, would be lost again. They had no men to throw into the line, and so they had to give up the ground they had won with such an effort, because even now the high command was not willing to risk more men. Kippenberger and the others knew at that moment that Brigadier Puttick, by refusing to commit his forces, was accepting defeat. And Puttick was already planning to move south and let the Germans have the whole area.

General Freyberg, too, had accepted defeat on Crete. He was now thinking about withdrawal southward, and ultimately withdrawal from the island of all who could make it.

It was not yet the end of the fighting on Crete, but the high command had given up all hope, and so there was nothing the fighting men could do.

CHAPTER 16

Battle

In London and Cairo on May 26, 1941, the political and military leaders of Britain were still talking about victory in Crete, but General Freyberg knew that he was looking into the face of defeat no matter what he did now. It did not matter that there were still far more Britons, Australians, New Zealanders and Greeks on the island than Germans. The Luftwaffe controlled the skies absolutely, and thus prevented the resupply and reinforcement of Crete.

General Wavell had already told General Freyberg that no merchant ship could survive within fifty miles of the island. That meant that the only help Freyberg could expect was what the Royal Navy was able to do at night, while the possession of Maleme airfield meant the Germans could bring in as many troops as they needed, as well as artillery and other weapons. At that one airfield, the Germans were bringing in 3,000 men per day, plus ammunition and supplies. It was true that the German troops fighting elsewhere than the Maleme area were still in difficulties, but any victories the British might score elsewhere would not affect the balance. General Student knew that he had already won the battle of Crete. His concern after a week of fighting was for the fate of his troops at Réthimnon and Iráklion. The Germans now had about 8,000 fighting men in the line, with more coming in every daylight hour.

Having guessed wrong about the importance of the air fields in the beginning, and having failed to hold the Maleme airfield, there was now nothing the British could do but fight a battle that must end in defeat, or else withdraw the troops from Crete. Freyberg's immediate concern was to make a retreat covered by a rear guard, and then move the troops out from a port to

Egypt, saving as many men as possible. As he told General Wavell that day, it was impossible to save the whole force. The only organized infantry troops he now had who were not too exhausted to fight were the Welch Regiment and the commandos. He expected Suda Bay to be attacked by a strong German force within a matter of hours. He also told Wavell that day that he was planning an evacuation from Sfakia.

Just now, the most important thing was to avoid being surrounded and trapped. Freyberg also wanted to establish a new defense line temporarily south of Canea to cover the unloading of stores from the destroyers that night.

Cairo had promised him two destroyers loaded with food and ammunition for the night of May 26. He wanted to move the food and ammunition to the village of Stilos, and then withdraw south to Sfakia and Port Loutro. But he could not move until he got answers to his messages to General Wavell, and he was not getting them. At Cairo, the Middle East staff was finding it hard to come to grips with the idea that the battle for Crete was lost.

General Ringel, the German commander, now saw that by capturing the village of Stilos, six miles from Suda Bay on the road to the port of Sfakia, he could encircle the British at Suda and Canea and at the same time rescue the Germans fighting at Réthimnon.

General Freyberg decided that his troops must hold a line west of the Kladiso River (which was west of Canea) for at least twenty-four hours. The Australians would hold the left side, while the center would be filled by the Suda Brigade of 2,000 men. On the right, the reserve force would hold the line. This force consisted of about 1,250 men from three units, the Welch Regiment, the Northumberland Hussars, and the Rangers. The reserve would be commanded by Brigadier Inglis.

Inglis then returned to divisional headquarters and told Brigadier Puttick of these plans. Puttick was distressed, because he thought the line would break before the twenty-four hours were up. He wanted to argue with General Freyberg, but there was no way to do it but in person, since communications had broken down. Nor was there any transportation available at divisional headquarters to take him to the force headquarters, four miles away at Suda Point, on the southern shore of the bay. So Brigadier Puttick was forced to walk.

An hour later, by chance, Brigadier Puttick ran into General Freyberg as he was passing through Suda. He suggested that the force withdraw to Suda immediately and hold the position there. But the problem was that if the troops moved to Suda, the Germans could come up within a mile of the quay where the destroyers would be landing their supplies. So Puttick was overruled and returned to his headquarters, where he had the disquieting news that the Germans were on the move around the left flank of the British, and that the Fifth Brigade was in danger of encirclement.

It was late afternoon by this time. West of the Kladiso River, the British troops were under heavy fire from the fresh Germans with their many mortars. The Germans were also moving through the foothills against the Greeks up there. But the line held that afternoon in spite of almost constant air attack from Me-109s. In one strafing pass, a German fighter killed fifteen men who had taken shelter in a gully.

General Weston was put in command of the western front that night, and he would be in charge the next day of the rearguard action that should let the majority of the troops escape towards Sfakia. Shortly before six o'clock that evening, Weston went to New Zealand divisional headquarters to confer with Puttick, and found the brigadier in a dither, convinced that the British line was breaking up. This danger was also indicated by Brigadier Vasey, who indicated that he should withdraw his troops to a point east of Suda Bay. Since Weston had no authority to make such a decision, he went in search of General Freyberg, but did not find him until well after nine o'clock that night. Freyberg was not impressed by Brigadier Puttick's worries. He issued a series of orders commanding the Australians, who were about to evacuate their position, to hold the line, and telling the New Zealand troops also to hold.

That night, the minelayer *Abdiel* and the destroyers *Hero* and *Nizam* came in to Suda Harbor bringing supplies and more Commandos, whose force had now risen to 800 men. The newcomers were told as they disembarked that they had to get out of the bay area by dawn or they would surely be attacked by the Luftwaffe. They were also told that Crete was lost and that their task now would be to become part of the rear guard to help the evacuation from the other side of the island.

General Freyberg than ordered ten tons of rations sent to Lieutenant Colonel Campbell, who was fighting so valiantly and successfully at Réthimnon. He was already planning to extricate Campbell and his men when the time came for the evacuation of the island, but he did not say anything to anyone about this because of the negative effect it would have on morale.

When General Freyberg arrived back at his headquarters after midnight, he had some responses to his messages to Cairo, but no replies to his questions. Instead of addressing the question of evacuation of Crete, General Wavell was sending him another general, General J. F. Evetts, who was an expert in tank warfare. Wavell was also suggesting that the forces retreat to Réthimnon and hold the eastern part of the island. Wavell still did not understand what the possession of the airfield plus the power of the Luftwaffe meant, lessons that Freyberg had now finally learned.

Within the hour, Freyberg had sent an answer to Wavell. The Réthimnon garrison, he said, was cut off by roadblocks held by the Germans. He had lost almost all of his artillery because he had no gun tractors to move them out of position to follow a retreating force. Although the "ration strength" of his force seemed large, most of the troops he had left had no arms and did not know how to fight infantry battles anyhow. The morale of his force was now very bad, largely because of the unremitting daily attacks of the Luftwaffe. The plan to withdraw to Réthimnon would lead to total disaster. The only way to save any of his force was to move them at night to the beaches, preferably in the south, and hide them during the day, to be taken off at night. He could not use any tanks if they sent them. The tanks would not last an hour under attack from the Luftwaffe. He could use some more trained troops to help with the rear guard. What they really needed, and had needed all along, was air support from the RAF.

Brigadier Puttick was dithering again. He remained convinced that an immediate withdrawal was all that would save his troops from destruction. He tried to get in touch with General Freyberg, but could not find him. He tried to get in touch with General Weston, under whose orders he had been placed, but could not find him, either. He waited. All sorts of dire thoughts seemed to pass through his head, including the fear that Weston had not been in touch because he had been killed. This could go on only so long, and at ten-thirty Puttick summoned his courage and, in violation of his orders, he ordered a retreat to begin at eleven-thirty.

A few minutes later he had news from the brigade that Freyberg had just ordered the Nineteenth Brigade to stand fast at all costs. He did not countermand his orders to the troops, but now stood in open violation of orders. So the New Zealands, the Australians, the Maoris, and the Greeks all began to retreat. But meanwhile the reserve was being sent to relieve them. The reserve was being moved into position beyond the Canea Bridge. Their commander, Brigadier Inglis, was not with them. He was retreating to Stilos.

The Rangers and the Hussars took up positions close to the river, and the Welch Regiment moved out into the olive trees and the ridges to occupy the trenches which had been prepared earlier. Soon they were scattered over a large area a mile beyond the bridge, with the right flank on the sea and the left flank across the Alikianou road. They stumbled over bodies—German, Greek, and New Zealander—but did not see a living soul.

By this time, the first of the retreating troops from Suda were marching along the mountain road to Sfakia, retreating as fast as they could go, while in London, Prime Minister Churchill was composing a message to General Wavell saying that it was essential for him to win a victory in Crete and exhorting him to give all the aid he could.

As dawn came, the troops of the reserve began to encounter Germans. At seven o'clock in the morning, the Messerschmitt 109 fighters arrived and began scouring the banks of the river looking for targets. They did not find much to shoot at. The reserve troops were well concealed.

Five German regiments were now ready to make the assault on Suda. Part of the Storm Regiment was astride the coast road, and the 120th Mountain Regiment, the Third Parachute Regiment, the 141st Mountain Regiment, and the Eighty-fifth Mountain Regiment were all ready to march.

It took the Germans some time to realize that the New Zealanders had withdrawn. At 7:30 A.M. they began to advance toward the head of Suda Bay to cut off the retreat through the olive groves. At 8:30 A.M., General Ringel ordered a general assault backed by his many mortars and heavy machine guns.

Now the men of the British reserve force, about 1,200 in

all, faced about 5,000 Germans who were moving on their front and on the left flank, where the New Zealand regiment was supposed to be. But there was no one there, and although Lieutenant Colonel A. Duncan, the field commander of the reserve, tried with his radio to raise General Weston but could not, nor could he get any information from anyone. The reserve force had been abandoned by the retreating Puttick. Weston had quit, too. He had abandoned his headquarters and was in retreat, heading for the Sfakia road. Behind him, he had left no instructions for the reserve force. Nor had anyone else.

The Germans now advanced, calling for Stukas to bomb the British positions. The scattered companies were swiftly overrun, and fire came in on them from all sides. Runners carrying messages from beleaguered units to Lieutenant Colonel Duncan were killed one after the other, and the messages of woe did not get through.

Duncan was in his command post under the river bank about a hundred yards from the bridge. He could tell from the sounds of battle that the German mortars and Spandau machine guns were winning. He decided to bring his two companies back from the left flank, and got orders through to them. Men came running in groups, charging through the trees and stopping to fire at the pursuing enemy, then to stumble on. Duncan told the survivors to go through Canea and reorganize on the Suda road.

As the survivors moved along the road, they were ambushed by German machine guns, but they kept moving in small groups through the trees, until finally they came to what had been General Weston's headquarters. There a line of Maoris and Australians was holding, and had just defeated a battalion of the German 141st Mountain Regiment, killing 300 of them and sending the rest running.

About 400 of the 1,200 men of the reserve force managed to make this line, squirming out of the trap their own commanders had set for them, and sent them into alone, without support or information.

Lieutenant Colonel Duncan stayed behind at his command post near the Kladiso bridge. The Germans were converging on him. The British turned their machine guns around to face the enemy. Soon their number was reduced to fifty, and then, in a wild fight, the Germans came down on them. Four British soldiers were taken prisoner. All the other men died.

About 200 of the Welch Regiment fought their way with Bren guns and grenades and rifle through the main streets of Suda town. Brigadier Hargest, who was still at the Weston headquarters, watched the fighting in dismay, and saw the Germans annihilate the Welch as they came through the town. "Whoever sent them should be shot," he said. He did not know that no one had sent them, no one had informed them, no one had helped them. They had been abandoned by their senior officers, who were busy moving along the road to Sfakia to save themselves.

In the confusion, General Ringel found it hard to figure out what the British were doing. He assumed that the main British force was still ahead of him in Canea. It was about noon before he realized that the British were abandoning Canea and Suda Bay and that they had, in fact, already abandoned their rear guard. Then he sent troops urgently forward to the head of the bay. They arrived and cleaned out the whole area, but took very few prisoners. Most of the British had fallen in battle.

The Germans marched their prisoners of war into the ruins of Canea. The Italians came out of their prison camp at last, and German prisoners, some of them held by the British for a week, joined the victorious troops in the town square.

And in the wreckage of the British army, on the road to Sfakia, General Weston had the temerity to approach General Freyberg and suggest that he surrender the whole force to the Germans.

CHAPTER 17

Fighting Retreat

On the afternoon of May 27, General Wavell finally bowed to the inevitable and announced to London that Crete had been lost and that all that remained was to try to extricate as many British troops as possible from the wreckage. This news was greeted grimly at No. 10 Downing Street, and destroyed whatever was left of Prime Minister Churchill's esteem for Wavell. Ten hours passed before Wavell had a reply to that message. The War Cabinet met and was told that all hope of success had ended. The navy agreed to rescue as many men as possible, and that message was sent to Wavell.

The permission to break off the battle was sent to General Freyberg. Of course his brigadiers had already broken off the battle many hours before and were in retreat across the mountains. Freyberg did not then know the extent of the rout that had taken place. He sent a message to Lieutenant Colonel Campbell, telling him to break contact with the enemy at Réthimnon and make his way to Sfakia. He did not know that the New Zealand Brigade and the Australians had withdrawn hours before. It was clear that the Welch Regiment had been destroyed, but he did not quite know how. He did not know what had happened to General Weston, who had simply disappeared, and was now to be found south on the road to Sfakia. There was no news at all from what had been the front line, and he did not know that the whole of it as far as the end of Suda Bay had been overrun by the five German regiments. So that night, General Freyberg himself set out for Sfakia, ignorant of the fact that most of his orders had been ignored.

The Australians were astride the road to Sfakia near the Suda

Bend, and the New Zealanders kept a gap from appearing as far as the foothills. Weston had advocated that they cut and run, telling them that morning that they were fools to stay on and fight. But they had stayed, and thus they had saved the four hundred men of the reserve who had gotten out of the trap left for them by General Weston.

Now thousands of Britons and Australians and New Zealanders were marching on the long weary road to Sfakia. The Australians and the New Zealanders, now, with the loss of the reserve, the rear guard, began to make their way along the road. By dawn, they had reached Stilos, which the first of the retreat had reached almost a day before. At the very end of the line were the commandos, fighting the last rearguard actions. That night the Germans were not very aggressive, and in the early hours of the morning, the commandos retired along the winding road. They were joined by three tanks which had been brought by ship down from Iráklion, and these tanks discouraged the Germans from attacking.

By dawn on May 28, none were left west of Suda save the dead, the captives, the wounded, and the Germans. Some of the wounded were still concealed and would try to escape their enemies. Some lay in the open and suffered from the heat and from thirst. Some were captured. Many died of their wounds.

The Germans still did not suspect that the British might be heading south to escape by sea. General Ringel was still trying to finish up the advance along the coast road. He would pursue the British through Réthimnon to Iráklion, and rescue his own Germans trapped at these two places. General Ringel formed a task force and sent it up the road to Réthimnon, with another regiment of Mountain troops on the right flank and more troops to guard the coast on the left and clear the Akrotiri peninsula.

Even though the British were retreating all day long on May 27 across the road to Sfakia, the Germans did not know it. The major reason was that the Luftwaffe, which had been their eyes for so long on Crete, had now been sharply diminished. When supreme headquarters in Berlin learned that the crisis on Crete had ended and that victory was a matter of time, it had begun withdrawing Luftwaffe units to send them to Russia for the coming invasion. By the afternoon of the twenty-seventh, only a few Me-109s remained in the Cretan skies—too many for the British by far, but not enough to pay much attention to what was going on in the mountains and toward the south. On the morning of May 28, there were only a handful of Luftwaffe planes cruising the Cretan skies, and, as their pilots had observed from the beginning of the battle, the British were masters at concealment.

Three reinforced German battalions had been sent east into the mountains to cut the British off at Stilos. They had been long delayed by the valiant Eighth Greeks, and when the first detachment arrived to climb the ridge west of Stilos early on the morning of May 28, it was too late. Almost all the British who were going to get out had arrived. Two companies of the Twenty-third Battalion were roused and came to the top of the ridge. From behind a stone wall, they ambushed the approaching Germans, waiting until they were about fifteen yards away before opening fire. They killed most of the Germans, and the rest beat a hasty retreat.

Thus far, the exception to the retreat to Stilos was the Maori unit. It had been selected to be the last of the rearguard, and it fought down by Suda for six hours on the morning of the twenty-eighth. Then, when they could see an unbroken column of Germans passing east along the coast road, the Maoris broke off and withdrew in a wide arc to the southeast.

The thirty-mile road between Stilos and Sfakia was filled with retreating British. In the van were the hangers-on, those troops from Suda who had been doing nothing but waiting for transport to Egypt. They had no arms and no leaders. When daylight came, they moved warily, keeping to the sides of the road and looking upward for the dreaded wings of the Luftwaffe. But this day they did not see them very often. When the planes did come, in the stillness the sounds of their engines betrayed their coming, and the men were able to take shelter well before they arrived overhead. The pilots looked down to see empty stretches of road.

General Freyberg observed the retreat and noted that in the main it was conducted by a disorganized rabble. That was what impressed him most: the disorganization and lack of control. In a sense, this was the hallmark of the whole British effort in Crete—disorganization and lack of control all the way through, from start to what was now nearly the finish.

That day, General Freyberg set up his new headquarters in a cave in the cliff near Sfakia, and began to make arrangements for the evacuation of the British troops. The road came down to the sea from the mountains, passing through a narrow pass, then down onto a green plain. The general ordered troops to guard the pass and, if necessary, fight a rearguard action to protect the plain. He gave the Fourth Brigade the task of protecting the plain itself against possible parachute landings.

Back at Stilos, the last of the British, the New Zealand Fifth Brigade, and the Australians faced the decision of staying there for the day—and undoubtedly being attacked by a far superior German force—or moving out in daylight and running the danger of attack by the Luftwaffe while on the road. They decided to face the uncertainties of the road rather than the certainty of an attack from which they might not recover. So at ten o'clock on the morning of May 28, they moved out through the barren foothills.

The men were nearly exhausted, having been fighting for more than a week, with very little sleep or food. They marched and they listened for the deadly sound of airplane engines. But the sound did not come. Miraculously, it seemed, the Luftwaffe did not put in an appearance that day.

Six miles from the village of Babali Hani, the soldiers entered a small valley with olive trees and oaks that gave shelter from the blazing Cretan sun. When they reached the village, the valley widened out to be more than a mile wide, and here the rearguard troops established their defensive position. They had started from Suda with three tanks, but two of them had broken down and so had been destroyed. That afternoon the Commandos and the Australians fought an engagement with the first German troops to reach Stilos. After driving the Germans off, the Australians retreated down the road toward Sfakia, the very last of the British line. They marched all night, and finally came to the defense line of the Fourth Brigade on the Askifou plain.

Two groups of British troops remained on the western side of Crete, the garrisons at Iráklion and Réthimnon. On May 27, the Iráklion garrison waited for an attack that the Germans were obviously developing. From Cairo, Middle East headquarters told the men at Iráklion to prepare to evacuate. Warships would come in at midnight and leave at 3 A.M. to take out 4,000 troops. That meant that only the British and Australians at Iráklion would be taken out, leaving the Greeks and the Cretans—who had staked their lives with the British—to shift for themselves.

At dawn on May 28, Brigadier Chappell ordered his men to begin preparing to move out. They wrecked their vehicles and set timed charges in their supply dumps. The Luftwaffe sent a few aircraft to bomb the area, but the Germans on the ground did not attack. As darkness fell, the soldiers began to file down toward the harbor through the ruined city, which had been so thoroughly bombed by the Luftwaffe earlier.

Three cruisers left Alexandria early on the morning of May 28, the *Ajax*, *Dido*, and *Orion*, but on the way they were attacked by the Luftwaffe, and the *Ajax* was damaged and had to return to Egypt. The destroyer *Imperial* suffered a near miss from a bomb, but kept on with the mission. So there were two cruisers left to make the evacuation, escorted by six destroyers. There were no further problems, and they pulled into Iráklion harbor that night.

The cruisers stayed out in the deep water, and the destroyers ferried the men from the quay to the bigger ships. At three-twenty on the morning of May 29, they sailed. The Germans were unsuspecting. But a few miles outside the harbor, the steering of the *Imperial* failed, and she almost collided with the *Dido* and then with the *Orion*. Admiral Rawlings, who was in command, ordered the destroyer *Hotspur* to take all the men off the *Imperial* and to sink her. There was no time to waste on cripples. The flotilla sailed on, and shortly after first light the *Hotspur* caught up, having sent the *Imperial* to the bottom.

The delays brought them to the Kaso Straits in broad daylight, and as expected, in these narrow waters they came under attack from the Luftwaffe. The destroyer *Hereward* was sunk. The men in the water were strafed by a Stuka dive bomber, but the survivors were rescued by Italian motor torpedo boats. Later in the morning the *Dido* and the *Orion* were both bombed and the captain of the *Orion* was killed. Later in the morning, the ships were attacked again by Stukas, and one bomb went through the bridge into the stokers' mess deck, killing more than 250 of the crew and passengers and wounding nearly 300.

The Luftwaffe attacks continued for eight hours, until the ships neared the Egyptian shore. They entered Alexandria harbor at eight o'clock that night. Of the 4,000 troops who had gone aboard the ships, 800 had been killed by the Luftwaffe on the way back to Egypt.

* * *

At Réthimnon, Lieutenant Colonel Ian Campbell and his Australians were still fighting. On May 27, they made an attack towards Periviola. They still had two tanks, but the first was hit by a mortar round and burst into flame and the second struck a land mine, lost a track, and stopped. The infantry, however, penetrated the German perimeter, but all the eight men who did were killed.

On the night of May 28, the Australians attacked again on both sides of the road to Perivolia, but suffered heavy casualties, and the Germans held their position. The British had now reduced the Germans to one single road block. They expected to capture that soon unless the Germans were reinforced, because the Germans had no heavy weapons and very few grenades.

Time was running out for Campbell, but he knew nothing about it. He had not received any messages from General Freyberg. The wireless set at Sfakia was unable to get a signal across the mountains. There was no word from Cairo. Campbell learned on May 29 that the situation in Crete was "extremely serious"—from a broadcast of the BBC. He also learned from the Greeks nearby that a large German force was approaching from the direction of Iráklion. And he calculated that he now had food to last his men for only one more day.

That night of the twenty-ninth, every twenty minutes a beach patrol flashed a message out to sea for the Royal Navy. But there was no Royal Navy about, and there was no reply, The Germans now had been able to bring tanks into Crete, and on the morning of May 30, three tanks, accompanied by infantry and motorcylcle troops and artillery, moved in on Campbell's force. His men were exhausted and hungry. They had been on half rations for three days, and they were nearly out of ammunition.

Sfakia was a three-day march across the mountains. Campbell told his officers the facts, and that they were free to try to make it to Sfakia if they thought they could. Then he tied a white towel to the end of a stick and walked out to meet the Germans.

CHAPTER 18

Evacuation

On May 28, General Freyberg made his plans for the evacuation of the troops from Sfakia. One thousand men were to be taken off that night, 6,000 on the following night, 3,000 on the night of May 30, and 3,000 on the night of May 31. That was the plan, but Freyberg did not really believe his rear guard could hold off the Germans until the thirty-first. As for fighting men, he estimated that only about 2,000 men remained with weapons and capability of fighting. They had three field guns. He intended to concentrate on evacuating the fighting troops on May 29, which he really believed would be the last night on which rescue would be possible.

Following the costly rescue of the troops at Iráklion, the Royal Navy was very nervous about the Sfakia operation, expecting heavy losses in ships and men. But Admiral Cunningham insisted that they must not let the army down. "It takes three years to build a ship," he said. "It will take three hundred years to build a new tradition."

At about midnight on May 28, as the battered ships of Admiral Rawlings' fleet were reaching Iráklion, four destroyers arrived off the shore of Sfakia. By 3 A.M. 1,100 men had been taken aboard the ships.

Freyberg had given command of the military operations to General Weston, while he supervised the evacuation. Weston protested that he wanted his men evacuated. And because he did nothing, men began plundering the supply dumps, until guards were posted. Then rations were issued to the fighting men in very small quantities. That was all they would get during the next three days.

General Freyberg's apprehensions about the possibilities of

a massive attack by the Germans were premature, as it turned out. The German high command in Berlin considered the Crete campaign to be ended, and believed that only mopping up and arranging for orderly occupation of the island remained to be done. Many of the troops were now moved out and sent to the eastern front. General Student went east with a heavy heart, still worrying about the men at Réthimnon and Iráklion.

General Ringel's men moved slowly along the Sfakia road, not wanting to waste men on a frontal assault, but bringing up machine guns and outflanking the defenders, who then moved back a bit and held again while the Germans moved again to outflank them. It was a slow business, and it gave the British more time. On May 29, the troops in the pass rebuffed a German attack in a series of small actions fought by the Eighteenth and Twenty-third battalions with three light tanks and three Bren carriers. Behind them were about 8,000 stragglers, in what was known as Rhododendron valley. Separated from the original units, they were now organized into groups of fifty for purposes of supply and discipline. That first night, some of them went aboard the ships, while the others waited patiently, hopeful now of getting out of Crete alive.

On the second night of the evacuation, Rear Admiral E. King arrived off Sfakia with eight cruisers and destroyers, and took from the shore 6,000 passengers. This time the navy had coverage from the RAF from dawn onward, and all the ships reached Alexandria safely without the loss of a man.

On the third day, General Freyberg was ordered to leave the island and told that a flying boat would be sent for him. He handed over command of his 7,000 man rear guard to General Weston and left, asking Cairo to send more ships to take the rest of the men off on the night of May 31.

That day of the thirtieth, a German patrol penetrated to within a few yards of the cave in the mountainside where force headquarters was located, but British infantry soon drove it off. By the time it grew dark the rear guard had moved to a position a mile above the end of the road, except for two battalions of Australians and one battalion of Royal Marines, who held the last post farther back.

At eleven o'clock that night, General Freyberg and his staff boarded the flying boat and left. On this night, four destroyers were sent to Sfakia, but two of them did not make it. The *Kandahar* developed engine trouble and the *Kelvin* was bombed, so they went back to Alexandria empty. The *Napier* and the *Nizam* took off 1,400 men, including most of the survivors of the Fourth New Zealand Brigade.

On May 31, the British retained their perimeter, with the Australians, the marines and the New Zealand Twenty-first Battalion guarding the ridge and the other troops moving down the mountain to Sfakia. The Germans made no progress, and the Luftwaffe planes that came over to bomb and strafe did not hit much of anything. British concealment was still excellent.

At four o'clock in the afternoon, General Weston reported to Cairo that about 9,000 troops remained on Crete.

But now the Royal Navy suddenly balked at sending more cruisers to Crete for the evacuation and Peter Fraser, the prime minister of New Zealand, who was still in Egypt, went to see Admiral Cunningham and made a personal plea for more ships. Cunningham then sent the cruiser *Phoebe* back to Crete and she picked up another 1,500 men.

So the evacuation continued, with five ships going to Sfakia on the night of May 31. But Admiral Cunningham announced that this would be the last trip, because the Mediterranean Fleet had been sharply reduced by losses and the need for repairs of some vessels. General Weston was still hoping that the evacuation would continue on the night of June 1, but Wavell had to tell him it would not.

This news was passed to London, where Prime Minister Churchill personally intervened with the Admiralty, asking that the remaining men be saved. But when the London admirals were in touch with Admiral Cunningham he was not persuaded. All available air cover had to be used at Tobruk. Cunningham was determined to limit his losses, and he remembered only too well what had happened at Iráklion. In and around Crete he had lost 2,000 men. So Cunningham decided to abandon the men remaining on that embattled island.

By six o'clock on the night of May 31, General Weston knew the facts. He asked General Wavell what action he should take, since there would be no rescue. General Wavell did not reply, shirking the responsibility of command, so General Weston had to make the decision himself.

Weston decided that the New Zealand Fifth Brigade and the Australians would be rescued. The marines, the Commandos and a few of the miscellaneous troops would go. But the rest would have to surrender, and one of the commando colonels was told to make contact with the Germans to that end as soon as the ships left.

In the final hours, as the men began to learn that there would be no more evacuation, a sort of wild panic seized the troops who were destined to be left behind. Some wrapped themselves in bandages and limped down to the docks, pretending to be walking wounded. Others blocked the way of the weary Australians as they came down from the mountaintop, and the last Australian battalion was delayed until it was too late to get away.

The Germans were in no hurry to close in. The commander divided his force that day, and sent two elements in wide flanking movements. By the evening of May 31, neither group had reached the shore. Seeing so many men in the Sfakia area, the German commander decided that it would be suicidal to attack without artillery and air support, and for these he must wait. So on June 1 there was no attack at all.

General Weston left with the last ship, and leaving behind him an order with Lieutenant Colonel Young of the Commandos. It read:

"The position must be considered in the light of the following facts.

There are no more rations available and men have had no food for three days.

The wireless set can only last a few hours and the risk of waiting for further instructions from headquarters Middle East Command cannot be accepted.

The decision to give priority in withdrawal to fighting troops has reduced numbers below the minimum necessary for resistance.

No more evacuation is possible.

You will collect as many senior officers as possible and make known to them the contents of this order.

You are ordered to make contact with the enemy and arrange capitulation."

June 1 dawned and the sun came out. By that morning, everyone on the island knew that the remainder of the British force had been deserted. Some men set out, without sufficient fuel, in several motor boats, to try somehow to make the African coast. Some began marching eastward down the coast. But most simply sat and stared.

At about nine o'clock, the Germans began to come out of the mountains. But then the Luftwaffe came again, with four Stuka dive bombers and four Me-109s. They bombed and strafed the troops down on the shore, killing British and German troops alike. Then they left, and the Germans began to collect their prisoners and march them back over the pass to the north shore and captivity.

CHAPTER 19

Aftermath

With the fall of Yugoslavia and Greece and then Crete, Hitler had secured his southern flank. Now most of the troops that he had concentrated in the Balkans could move north and east to participate in the war against Russia. He no longer had to worry, either, about possible British air raids on the Ploesti oil fields. The British no longer had any bases from which they could reach them.

Admiral Erich Raeder, the chief of the German navy, was pressing for stronger action in the Mediterranean. On May 30, he asked Hitler to start a decisive offensive against Egypt and Suez. In Africa, General Erwin Rommel echoed these sentiments. Raeder predicted that such a move would be more deadly to Britain than the capture of London. A week later, Raeder gave Hitler a memorandum prepared by the Navy Operations Division discussing the importance of the Mediterranean and the importance of stepping up the war there. But Hitler had his mind made up, and would not budge from the position that Operation Barbarossa must take precedence and that Russia must be conquered before the resources would be available to move more strongly in Africa.

The British had suffered sharp defeats in Greece and Crete, and Prime Minister Churchill was subjected to a hail of criticism in the House of Commons. Not only had Greece been indefensible from the beginning, as General Wavell had originally held, but Crete's defense had never been planned or the defense installations strengthened. The first responsibility was Churchill's. He was the man who had insisted against all advice on going into Greece when his advisors told him repeatedly that Britain did not have the manpower available in the south to stand off the Germans if they attacked. But responsibility for the second disaster, that of Crete, had to rest with General Wavell, who had ignored Churchill's demands that the defense of Crete be strengthened in the six months before the actual attack. Nor could the chiefs of the Imperial General Staff escape their responsibility for the decision that the airfields of Crete were not to be destroyed. General Freyberg had to be responsible for failing to recognize the value of the airfields to the Germans and their absolute need to have at least one airfield to make their airborne invasion successful.

The German success in Crete aroused much speculation in Britain and abroad about further airborne operations. But the Germans knew, if no one else did, how nearly they themselves had escaped disaster. It had only been averted because of a series of bad judgments and misunderstandings by the British. First, Brigadier Hargest would not reinforce Lieutenant Colonel Andrew when he needed it. Then Andrew misread the strength of the Germans around Hill 107 and abandoned it to the enemy. Thus, the vital airfield was lost because no one would make the decision to counterattack in the three nights that it was possible to do so and win.

In Cairo, a special commission of inquiry was established to discover what had happened on Crete. The commission found that there had been much dereliction in the matter of the defenses, a finding that so annoyed Generals Wavell and Freyberg that the results were suppressed.

The fighting on Crete had cost the British more than 18,000 men, almost 12,000 of them prisoners of war, with about 1,800 killed and 1,800 wounded. The British navy had lost more than 1,800 men killed in the Crete operations. The Greek and Cretan losses will never be known, but they were extremely high. The Germans had lost 6,000 men, with 4,000 of these killed. To the Germans, the Crete campaign was a serious setback. They lost more men killed in the first day's operations than they had lost in all the operations of the Wehrmacht up to that time. They lost half their entire parachute corps, and many bright young officers. The Germans then concluded that in any future airborne operations, absolute mastery of the air must be a prerequisite. In their minds, that was what had saved the Crete invasion. Hitler was so displeased with the high rate of casualties that he said the day of the parachute troops was over because it depended on surprise, and it was no longer possible to employ that element.

Another major factor in the defeat was the British failure at every stage of the fight to better their very bad communications. On several occasions, it would have been possible to have delivered radio equipment that should have been in place from the beginning, but no attempt was made to do so by Cairo, and no serious demands for radios were made by Freyberg or his brigadiers. For a nation that had just come through the Battle of Britain successfully largely because of the strength of the Royal Air Force communications, that communications failure in Crete was a serious indictment of the leadership.

At first the British feared that the example of Crete would soon be followed by parachute landings in Britain. The London newspapers speculated on parachute attacks. But on sober consideration, Peter Fraser told his New Zealanders who returned to Egypt that after Crete the Germans would never try parachute landings in Britain.

One aspect of the battle for Crete that was to have far-reaching consequences in the war was the attrition to the JU 52s in the air drops. Of 600 aircraft employed, 170 were lost or made useless for the future. The Luftwaffe had a shortage of transport craft anyhow, and this made it much worse. The effects were to be felt two years later at Stalingrad, when Goering could not make good his promise to supply the beleaguered German Sixth Army because of a shortage of aircraft.

General Student agreed with Admiral Raeder and General Rommel in wanting to move against Suez. His plan was to stage another air invasion of Cyprus, which would then be used as a point of departure for a paratroop attack on the Suez Canal. But Hitler rejected the plan, not only because he was concerned more with Russia, but also because of the heavy losses at Crete. Later, however, Student was able to persuade Hitler to adopt a plan for the capture of Malta. Student would command a combined German-Italian parachute force, consisting of his division, three additional regiments, and an Italian parachute division. The Italian navy would then bring in six to eight ordinary infantry divisions by sea. The plan was all set, Student thought, and he flew to Berlin for a final conference. The Fuehrer then had one of his lightning changes of mind and decided the plan would not do. It would be too expensive in terms of lives, and it might well go wrong. He was thinking about Crete again, and so the memory of Crete saved Malta.

Could Crete have been held, given the forces involved? Historian I. McD. G. Stewart considered that it could have been held, in spite of the appreciations later made by Wavell and Freyberg that it could not have been. The key to the fall of Crete was the abandonment of Hill 107 by the Twenty-second Battalion on the first night of the fighting.

The Germans understood the battle and the reasons for their victory much better than the British. They had not won the struggle so much as the British had lost it through inept leadership. That is what they told their prisoners of war: that the loss of Crete had not been through any failure by the soldiers but through the failure of the commanders. The British denied it, but it was true all the same.

Had the commanders been more aggressive, and had the island been held, Hitler would never have had the resources to try to take Crete again. Twelve days after the victory in Crete, he invaded Russia, and the long campaign of attrition of his Luftwaffe and his divisions began.

And of what particular value was Crete to the Germans?

First, it was an important support for General Rommel's operations in North Africa. Hitler considered the island very important in his defense of his southern extremity. In 1943, he transferred troops from the west to Greece in anticipation of Allied invasions of Crete and Greece, invasions that never happened but were part of a British deception scheme to hide the coming invasion of Italy.

When Italy was invaded, Hitler's concern for Greece and Crete increased. In the fall of 1943, several of his generals and Admiral Karl Doenitz urged the evacuation of Crete and the other Aegean islands because they were so costly to maintain. Hitler refused because of the political repercussions of such a move. Rumania, Bulgaria, and Hungary, all German allies, would have been distressed to see the Germans leave a vacuum to their south, and Turkey's neutralism might be lost if the Germans left the Aegean.

Both Hitler and Churchill were preoccupied with the Aegean. Churchill referred to it as the soft underbelly of Europe, and almost until the day of the invasion of France, he wanted to go into Europe through that back door. Hitler was afraid that the Allies would do just that, and begin to roll up his empire from the south.

As to Crete and the Cretans, once the Germans won their campaign, they did not forget that the Cretans had fought against them. The Cretans and Greeks had held the Germans at the port of Kisamos Kastelli for seven days, until the Germans brought a full battalion of troops to the port and then managed to land a few tanks. The Germans also found some bodies of their troops who had been mutilated, and so after the victory they shot two hundred Cretans in the town square of Kisamos Kastelli. And too soon the SS arrived, and a campaign of terror and murder began against the civil population.

Thus the Balkan blitzkrieg ended. In retrospect this adventure by Hitler had lasting consequences on the future of the war. Because he felt he had to go into Yugoslavia and Greece, Hitler had delayed the invasion of Russia, which was originally scheduled for May 15 and did not come about until June 22. Those weeks made an enormous difference, and may have saved the Soviet Union, because Hitler's forces were moving very fast through Russia that summer and were scarcely slowed down until rains came in mid-October. The mud was immediately followed by the first winter snows, and the Germans bogged down in a combination of mud, slush, and ice. By the end of November, the temperature had dropped to 20 degrees below zero Centigrade, and the German tanks were freezing up.

As for the British, the Greek and Crete campaigns marked a worsening of their position in Africa. Before Prime Minister Churchill insisted on the Greek campaign, the British in North Africa had been winning, and with a little more effort might have defeated the Italians before General Rommel could have gotten started with his very successful campaign. But when major forces were suddenly pulled away from the desert war and sent to Greece, the desert campaign had to be halted, and Rommel had his chance.

As commander-in-chief of the forces in the Middle East, General Wavell had four expeditions thrust upon him between the winter of 1940 and the middle of 1941. He had to intervene in Iraq, in Syria, and in Ethiopia. By the time of Crete, the Ethiopian campaign was nearly over, but in April a pro-German regime seized power in Iraq, and this threatened the British oil supply. The Iraqis might turn off the pipeline through which oil flowed to Haifa in Palestine. Wavell had to send troops to

Iraq, and this further depleted his forces. His reaction to the whole idea was negative, which made Prime Minister Churchill even less fond of him. But in the end, Wavell's troops reestablished a pro-British government and solved the problem of Iraq. This had scarcely occurred when the Vichy French forces in Syria began to show signs of pro-German activity. German planes were using Syrian airfields. So Wavell had to send an expeditionary force to fight a war he did not want. He did so, and in six days the British quelled the Vichy French.

But the Greek experience had cut the British African desert forces to one division, part of a British motorized division, and an Indian motorized brigade. Rommel had attacked in March and taken Benghazi in April and then Bardiyak and Sollum. He advanced toward Egypt and besieged Tobruk, which the British fortified because Wavell wanted to keep a threat on Rommel's flank. The siege of Tobruk was going on when Crete was attacked, and lasted until December 1941.

Meanwhile, Wavell mounted a counterattack against the Germans just after the fall of Crete. He had many matters on his mind, obviously, all during the ten-day battle for the island. By the end of it, his mind was in the desert. Prime Minister Churchill had been growing more and more vexed with Wavell, and the fall of Crete was the next-to-the-last straw. The last one was the failure of the counterattack against Rommel. It was very clear to all who knew that the Middle East command was spread too thin, and that the British would need to rearm and organize their armies in Africa much more thoroughly than they had been. But to Prime Minister Churchill, the principal problem was that Wavell was a loser. He decided to replace him with General Claude Auchinleck and did so on July 5.

General Auchinleck mounted an offensive in mid-November. His forces reoccupied Benghazi on Christmas Eve, after moving 300 miles. By the end of December, Rommel had retired to Al Agheila along the road to Tripoli but at the end of January he advanced again and reoccupied Benghazi and with the Italians occupied a line from Al Gazala on the coast to Bir Hacheim. The Allies hung onto Tobruk.

The desert line stayed where it was until the following May. Auchinleck's offensive was costly, his casualties amounted to 17,000 men. But the German and Italians lost twice as many, All the while, much of Rommel's air support came from Crete, where all three of the airfields were in use by the Luftwaffe.

Again in December, Auchinleck faced the same problems that had dogged General Wavell: shortages, particularly of men. When the Japanese attacked in December 1941, they threatened New Guinea and Australia, and two of Auchinleck's Australian divisions were shipped back home.

Rommel advanced rapidly in the desert and seemed to know all the British plans. In fact he *did* know, because the Italians had gotten into the American embassy in Rome and stolen the key to the "black code" which the American military attache in Cairo used to send his messages to Washington. The Italians were able to read the messages and pass the information to Rommel. It was months before the fact was discovered and the codes changed.

But Rommel bogged down for four months on the Al Gazala-Bir Hacheim Line, for two reasons. One was the determination of the British Royal Navy which kept sinking Rommel's supply ships. The second was the continued existence of the British air and naval base at Malta. It was this base that General Student thought he had an agreement to attack with his paratroopers in 1942 after Rommel made a trip to Germany to plead with Hitler for the occupation of Malta. Hitler did send a strong air fleet to destroy the Malta air base, but the island continued to hold out. Rommel said that Malta was preventing him from winning in Africa, so Hitler had agreed to the softening-up and then the parachute landing. In the end, however, as noted, he reneged on the agreement. And so Malta was saved, a part of the inheritance of Crete and the Balkan blitzkrieg.

NOTES

1 The Italians Start a War

In this chapter I relied on the Bitzes book, *Churchill and Shirer*, and also on conversations with George Weller, Pulitzer prize winning correspondent for the *Chicago Daily News* who covered the war in Greece and wrote a book about it, *A Crack in the Column*. Winston Churchill was most certainly the architect of the British intervention in Greece, which he insisted on over the advice to the contrary from his generals. Very early in the discussions, Wavell raised the point that the British could not possibly put enough men and equipment into Greece to stop a determined drive by the Germans, who had several hundred thousand soldiers in the Balkans, plus very strong elements of the Luftwaffe.

2 The Germans Strike

This chapter called upon the Bitzes book and Laird Archer's *Balkan Diary*, a personal account by an American businessman who was in Athens at the time of the German invasion. Also, Churchill was valuable for this as was MacIntyre. What astounded the world was the speed with which the Germans rolled up the defenses of Yugoslavia.

3 Defense of Crete

For this chapter, I depended on the Woollcombe book, Churchill, Arnold-Forster and Somerville's *World War II, Day by Day*, (Dorset Press 1989). It was unkind of the soldiers to refer to the Middle East Command as "the Muddle East" and the confusion was not entirely the fault of General Wavell, who had too many different responsibilities to carry out in the political and diplomatic fields as well as the military.

4 The Defenders

For the study of the defense and attack on Crete, the definitive work is I. McD. G. Stewart's *The Struggle For Crete*.

Most of the books written before this one were full of errors passed on almost from the beginning of the battle by sources in Cairo and London. Churchill was important here, as in the whole study of the Balkan blitzkrieg, and Arnold-Forster set the stage.

5   They Called It "Colorado"

The state of the defenses of Crete comes from Stewart and Woollcombe and Churchill, who had many misconceptions. The material about the Luftwaffe is from *The Luftwaffe* and from studies made for my Goering book.

6   The German Plan

The material about the Luftwaffe and the German plans comes from *The Luftwaffe*, and from Stewart. What was remarkable was that the Germans had so little concept of the strength of the British defenses. In terms of numbers of defenders, the British were very strong. Their weapons left a great deal to be desired, but the greatest problem, which had been true from the beginning when Churchill told Wavell to strengthen the Crete defenses, was leadership. It would be the great problem throughout the campaign and the real reason that Crete was lost to Britain.

7   The First Day—the Airborne Assault

The material for this chapter came from Stewart for the most part. I also consulted Buckley. The conclusions and inferences are my own.

8   The First Day—Down in the Valley

The chapter depended on MacIntyre, Buckley, Stewart and Spencer.

9   Iráklion

The source material is in the various books on the battle for Crete. The remarkable thing about the Iráklion situation was the complete isolation of Brigadier Chappell and his men from the realities of the action in the west. Certainly this was an indication of the important part that failure of British communications made in the course of the battle. German communications were excellent throughout.

10   The Réthimnon Airstrip

The brave battle of Lieutenant Colonel Campbell and his men is one of the high points in the story of the defense of Crete. Of the historians, Stewart is the most analytical and it was his conclusion that, had the entire defense been conducted with the aggressiveness of the Campbell operations, that the battle might have been won by the British at the critical juncture, the first and second nights.

11   The Battle Scene

The various histories, Woollcombe, and Churchill were consulted for this chapter.

12   The Long Night

This material comes from the Buckley, Spencer and Stewart histories of the battle for Crete. What seems inexplicable is the impression that Lieutenant Colonel Andrew had that his position on Hill 107 was desperate, when the indications are that his position was still strong and the German position was very weak that night.

13   The Germans at Maleme

The key to the battle, General Student learned on this first night, was the British abandonment of the height that controlled the Maleme airfield. Stewart discusses this in detail.

14   The Tide Changes

The detail of the battle is from the Stewart, Buckley, and Spencer histories. The references to the London view are dependent on Churchill.

15   Day of Battle

The German attack on Galatas was an attempt to take Suda in a hurry and thus control Suda Bay, preventing the Royal Navy from using it at night, and using it themselves to bring in supplies for the airborne troops.

16 Battle

What is so strange about the British military's failure to understand the vital nature of airpower in the battle of Crete is the fact that in Britain the leaders of the Royal Air Force understood it very well, and thus, logically, so should the British chiefs of staff. Why then the chiefs of staff told Wavell that he was *not* to destroy the Crete airfields begs belief. It is of a piece with General Freyberg's idea that the airfields were not in themselves important. His colossal lack of understanding must be regarded as a triumph for German propaganda, which deliberately built up in the British mind the impression that the German paratroop force was ten times as strong as it actually was.

17 Fighting Retreat

Almost until the last, Prime Minister Churchill and the War Cabinet thought that the battle for Crete was going well. This was a real failure in communication by General Wavell, but it is hard to blame him, because he knew Churchill's views and also stubbornness that sometimes made the Prime Minister refuse to listen to what he did not want to hear. As far as the retreat toward Sfakia was concerned, this seems to have been the best ordered part of the entire British defense effort, with the exception of the performances of the Campbell unit and the Maoris.

18 Evacuation

Roskill, my own *Hitler's War*, and the three histories of the battle for Crete were used in this chapter. The evacuation of Crete was not one of the Royal Navy's finest moments. In spite of everything but direct orders from London, Admiral Cunningham refused to go the last mile and take the men waiting on the beach at Sfakia to safety in Egypt. As it turned out, it would have been much easier than Cunningham believed, because the Luftwaffe by May 30 had all but disappeared from the island skies. Not entirely, as the merciless strafing of Germans and British alike on the shore that last day indicates. But the strength of the Luftwaffe was less than what it might have needed to do serious damage to Cunningham's ships.

19   Aftermath

My own *Hitler's War, Goering's war*, Churchill, and the Crete battle histories are the basic sources for this chapter. It became obvious to the German general staff within the year that a serious mistake had been made in attacking Crete instead of Malta. General Student pressed the case and thought he had won a victory with Hitler. But in 1943, when Student came to Berlin to make the plans for the assault on Malta, Hitler changed his mind. By that time his attention never wandered very far from the eastern front which had turned from a successful blitzkrieg of the Russians into a debacle.

BIBLIOGRAPHY

Arnold-Forster, Mark. *The World At War*, New York; Stein and Day, 1973.

Bitzes, John G. *Greece in World War II*. Manhattan, Kansas: Sunflower University Press, 1989.

Buckley, Christopher. *Greece and Crete, 1941*. London: Her Majesty's Stationer's Office, 1952.

Churchill, Winston S. *The Second World War*. Vols. II and III. London: Cassell, 1949, 1950.

Faber, Harald, ed. *Luftwaffe, a History*, New York: Times Books, 1977.

Hoyt, Edwin P. *Hitler's War*. New York: McGraw Hill, 1988. *Goering's War*. London: Robert Hale, 1989.

Liddell-Hart, B. H., ed. *The Rommel Papers*. New York: DaCapo Press, 1953.

MacIntyre, Donald. *The Battle for the Mediterranean*. London: Batsford, 1964.

Roskill, S. W. *The War at Sea*. Vol III. London: HMSO, 1961

Schirer, William L. *Rise and Fall of the Third Reich*. New York: Simon and Schuster, 1956.

Spencer, John Hall. *Battle for Crete*. London: Heinemann, 1962.

Stewart I. McD. G. *The Struggle for Crete*. Oxford: Oxford University Press. 1991.

Woollcombe, Robert. *The Campaigns of Wavell, 1939–43*. London: Cassell, 1959.

INDEX

Abdiel, 134
Africa, 6, 7, 19, 38, 40
air power: Britain, 28, 101;
    Germany, 28, 43, 101, 121,
    135, 151; Italy, 28
Ajax, 111, 143
Albania, 8, 11, 12, 17, 19, 21,
    22, 23, 35, 41; Greek
    withdrawal from, 32; Italian
    invasion of, 6, 11, 16
Aldridge, James, 17
Aliákmon Line, 24, 25, 27–28,
    30
Allen, J. M., 79, 105, 115
Andrew, L. W., 57–58, 76–79,
    80, 99, 103–06, 115, 151;
    withdrawal from Hill 107,
    80, 104, 105
Andros, 36
Antonescu, Ion, 19
Anzac Corps (Australia/New
    Zealand), 35, 36, 37
Archer, Laird, 26–27, 29,
    31
Ark Royal, 4, 5
Atlantic, Battle of, 1–5
Atlantis, 3

Auchinleck, Claude, 155, 156
Australian Sixth Division, 25
Azra, 23

Badoglio, Pietro, 12
Balkan League, 6
Battle of Atlantic, 1–5
Battle of Britain, 1, 117, 152
Bismarck, 3, 4–5; attack on, 5;
    sinking of, 5
Blenheim bombers, 32, 122
Brauchitsch, Walther von, 7
Brauer, Colonel, 88, 90–91,
    125
Brewster Buffaloe aircraft, 42
Britain, 10, 15; aid to Greece,
    providing, 8, 19, 21; Battle
    of, 1, 117, 152; defense of
    Crete, 38–44, 63; escort
    vessels, shortage of, 2–3;
    expectations of defense for
    Crete, 63; guarantees to
    Greece, 15; Joint Planning
    Staff, 22, 39; lack of
    knowledge of Crete, 43;
    reasons for failure in Crete,

163